MINISTRY LOVES COMPANY

MINISTRY LOVES COMPANY

A Survival Guide for Pastors

JOHN GALLOWAY JR.

Westminster John Knox Press
LOUISVILLE • LONDON

Book design by Sharon Adams
Cover design by Lisa Buckley
Cover illustration by Nancy Dawe

First edition
Published by Westminster John Knox Press
Louisville, Kentucky

This book is printed on acid-free paper that meets the American National Standards Institute Z39.48 standard. ♾

PRINTED IN THE UNITED STATES OF AMERICA

03 04 05 06 07 08 09 10 11 12 — 10 9 8 7 6 5 4 3 2 1

Library of Congress Cataloging-in-Publication Data

Galloway, John T.

    Ministry loves company : a survival guide for pastors / John Galloway, Jr.
      p. cm.
    ISBN 0-664-22584-5 (alk. paper)
      1. Pastoral theology. 2. Pastoral theology—Presbyterian Church. I. Title.

BV4011.3 .G35 2003
253—dc21

                                  2002027014

To
Susan

Contents

Foreword by John M. Buchanan ix

Acknowledgments xv

Introduction 1

I. Coming to Town

1. Family Reunion 9
2. Do Nothing 14
3. It's Not My Church 19
4. Have Patience 24

II. Convictions That Drive Us

5. Vision 33
6. Accountability 41
7. Reforming 47
8. Priorities 53

III. Company's Coming

9. Numbers 63
10. Administration 70
11. Parking 75
12. What's Your Competition? 81

IV. Conflict Happens

13. Conflict 89
14. The Tyranny of the Touchy 95
15. It's Not about Us 103

16. Coping   110
17. The Body of Christ   118

V. Commitment to Stewardship and Mission
18. Commitment   127
19. Knowing What People Give   134
20. The Mission Committee   141
21. Spiritual Renewal for the Sake of Mission   149
22. Money Follows Vision   156

Conclusion   165

Foreword

*P*eople often ask those of us who are ministers how and why we made our vocational decision. There is genuine curiosity behind the question most of the time, and also a suspicion that we must have had an intense religious experience, a moment of utter vocational clarity, when we heard God call our name and tell us to pack our bags and go to seminary. People who ask the question are often disappointed to know that ministers struggle with vocational decisions just like everybody else and, as a matter of fact, continue to think about the decision and make the decision to be a minister over and over again all their professional lives. There is also behind the question a sense that normally ambitious men and women would not decide on their own to be ministers out of all the vocational options open. I'll never forget meeting with the head of the political science department to discuss my senior project during the last semester of college. He asked me what I was planning to do next year. When I told him I thought I wanted to go to divinity school, he was shocked. "Why in the world would you do a thing like that?" he asked.

We do it because most of us come to the conclusion that we are "called" to be ministers. We remind ourselves that the word "vocation" itself comes from the Latin word "to call." Although we may use different language to describe it, and though we experience it differently, most of us believe that what we have decided to do with our lives was not the result solely of our own intellectual discernment. We also are inclined to see our vocation as a kind of gift from God.

For all those reasons we probably spend more time thinking about how we answer God's call, how we practice the profession of ministry, than any other professionals in our culture. Well, among the many books written on the subject over the years, this one is important. John Galloway Jr. loves what he does and understands it thoroughly. Moreover, he is a seasoned, experienced practitioner, whose ministry in several Presbyterian congregations is respected and recognized as a model for all of us.

There is an urgency about this book that responds to an urgent need. "Only about half of the . . . students at our seminaries are Presbyterian. Of them, only about half intend to enter the pastorate as pastor or associate pastor. Once in the parish, at least 20 percent will leave within the first five years" (Introduction, p. 2). Obviously, the mainline church in our day, in addition to its much-publicized decline in numerical strength and public influence, has a leadership crisis on its hands.

We need to do everything we can to understand our profession as thoroughly as possible and to build into the intellectual and practical preparation of ministers as much concrete experience and advice as possible. We must listen carefully to those who have practiced our profession with the energy, intelligence, imagination, and love each of us promises in our ordination vows. We can help one another, by sharing what we have learned and know, and by making available the creative thinking of the best among us. That is what John Galloway has set out to do—although his modesty would prevent him from claiming the expertise he clearly has and the respect he has earned.

His first image of a congregation as a family is most helpful. As I look back on my own forty-year ministry and my rough landing in my first congregation, I wish someone had told me that I had just arrived at a family reunion that had been going on for years before I showed up and would continue after I was gone, and that my job was to be a "reunion facilitator." In fact, I recall thinking of myself as the "great educator" who would lead my students from darkness to light, and the "great liberator" who, like Moses, would lead captive people out of bondage to the past into a glorious new freedom. It is no wonder that two of the ten or so pillar families were gone in the first six months. Most of us learn the hard way that a congregation is at least in part a family reunion. The fortunate among us are taught by a gracious, patient, and kind congregation that sees its mission in terms of completing the education of seminary graduates. When we learn, we fall in love and ministry begins to happen.

Galloway takes subtle aim at theological education by observing that before we begin our work as a reunion facilitator, we go to a school not to study how to do the work of "reunion facilitating" but other matters like the history of hotels and general weather conditions in New England. It is a sensitive and important issue. Just what constitutes appropriate preparation for ministry has been under careful scrutiny and discussion for a long time. No one seriously proposes that theological education should be less rigorous academically. An educated ministry is a defining characteristic of my own faith tradition. I personally wish theological education would be more demanding, seminaries more selective. I personally wish it were more, not less, difficult to complete the academic preparation the church has always said is the prerequisite for ordination. I also know, beyond a shadow of a doubt, that academic achievement alone, no matter how rigorous, is not sufficient preparation for parish ministry. The kind of theological education most of us experienced has not changed much in five hundred years: reading many books in order to write learned, heavily footnoted papers in theology, bible, history, and ethics, and achieving a minimal reading proficiency in Greek and Hebrew. Not for a minute do I want to lessen that. The ability to translate the first eighteen verses of the Gospel of John from Greek to English, and the ability to write a twenty-page comparison of the doctrine of the atonement in Thomas Aquinas, John Calvin, and Karl Barth, while perhaps deserving of academic honor and a coveted A, is not enough to help the young minister with her first funeral—for a church member who died suddenly and much too soon, leaving a wife and three small children. Nor will it help the pastor when his session, board of trustees, or executive committee becomes mired in conflict and grinds to a halt, with the atmosphere turning testy and sullen.

Galloway and others observe that sometimes young ministers conclude that the congregation is the enemy, an opponent to be overcome. It's no wonder, if no one ever told us that ministry is about people, real flesh-and-blood human beings, and a real human institution with a real history and real traditions and customs, and a very real propensity to act like "family," especially when a stranger with new academic credentials arrives, speaking in words nobody can understand, and starts trying to change things.

When you think about it, no other institution or profession would do that—regard academic preparation as adequate for full professional practice. Graduating from medical school and passing medical board examinations does not allow one to do open heart surgery. In fact, academic requirements lead to residency, a time of demanding, disciplined practice under the watchful eye of attending physicians. It is encouraging to see theological education move in the direction of incorporating hands-on experience in a parish setting into seminary curriculum. Planning, arranging, evaluating, and grading field experience takes time and precious resources and must happen in an intellectual environment that sometimes is loath to take it seriously. A graduate course in "Practical Theology" often turns out to be more "practical" than "theology." Graduates of one of our seminaries continue to regale their friends with stories of practicing baptisms in a classroom, using a life-size doll to learn the fine art of balancing a baby and the liturgy book while keeping one hand free to deliver water from the font to the infant's head. We laugh, of course, and yet the reality is that to pull it off on Sunday morning during worship—without dropping the baby—does require a little know-how.

The resolution to the quandary of whether or not practical academic courses belong in the academic curriculum is to understand that they fall into a different category of preparation for ministry. Furthermore, because they are the equivalent of rotations and residencies in medical education, the primary location for them is the congregation, not the classroom, and the primary teacher is an experienced pastor, not a tenured professor.

What we need is for the ecclesiastical structures responsible for ordaining to pay as much attention to practice as they do to academics. When, and how, and with whom, and with what measurable results a candidate for ordination did his or her residency, is at least as important as the grades he or she achieved in church history. That means that the church will have to change the way it thinks about ordination, get far more involved with theological education than it currently is, and come up with resources to find a new system of preparing for ministry. Fortunately, there are signs that both the church and the academy are ready and willing to begin thinking anew and, even more fortunately, that there are resources beginning to be available. The Lilly Endowment, for instance, is currently funding several congregation-based, two-year programs in residency in pastoral ministry. The program places seminary graduates in a "teaching parish" for two years of supervised practice in ministry.

John Galloway's book is brimming full of good advice for all of us, beginners, ministers entering a new ministry, and old-timers who, the author suspects, have given up on growing and have settled for waiting it out until they can cast their lot with their pension fund. For instance, I wish someone had told me that one of the things I must do on entering a new ministry with a new congregation is read old session and congregational meeting minutes as a way to learn about my new family and the ongoing family reunion I have been called to facilitate. What a great suggestion! Watching for lonely people in the coffee hour or organizing a group to do it is a trick I learned after years of observing the peculiar dynamic of community actually shutting out those who have come looking for it. Galloway describes it accurately. Church members are so glad to see one another and so eager to engage in conversation with church friends that a visitor finds it daunting, if not impossible, to break in. Oddly, the stronger the sense of community in a congregation, the less hospitable it is to the stranger for whom, after all, Galloway reminds us, the church exists in the first place. It doesn't have to be that way. Church people don't mean to exclude, and how I wish I had read Galloway's reminder decades ago! Hospitality, the church as the welcoming, open-armed, inclusive body of Christ: is there a more important ecclesiology for our time than that? The author reminds us that there is a renewed spiritual hunger and search for authentic spirituality going on in our culture and that the first thing we have to offer the world is the hospitality of Jesus. September 11, 2001, will remain throughout our lifetime as the day people of faith learned two critical lessons: about the religious diversity of our own culture and the suddenly smaller and more dangerous world we must share with people of faiths different from our own; and about the reality that religious zealotry, when combined with political and cultural ideology, is capable of indescribable evil. In the aftermath of September 11, people came to places of worship, almost instinctively, it seemed to me, because they knew that the hope of the world lies in an alternate vision of religion as welcoming, including, serving, loving.

"Family Reunion" is not, finally, an adequate metaphor for the church, at any level, not even the congregation. The time comes when we must leave the reunion to do the work our Lord calls us to do. Galloway reminds us that the church exists for the people who are not in it; exists for mission the way fire exists for burning. Survival alone is simply not a big enough purpose to energize the institution, nor is it big enough to sustain an individual ministry. We are called to be the body of Christ in the world and to do the work of his kingdom. Mission is not something a congregation does after it has paid all its bills and taken care of itself. Mission in the world is why it exists. Congregations that understand that about themselves will become lively, open, Spirit-filled, and, in my experience, compelling. It is and always has been difficult to ignore a Christian community that knows who it is and what it is for and then goes into the world and lives as Christ's own body.

There is a strong word here for the particular denomination the author loves at a particularly fragile moment in its long history. We are a denomination deeply divided, in danger of making idols of our ideological commitments, focused far more intently on our differences theologically than on the common faith that makes us one in spite of our differences. It is a prescription for schism, as our own Reformed history proves. The most important resource to help us bear with one another through this time, curiously, is the Reformed theological tradition itself. That tradition is based on the Reformation theme that human truth claims are limited, that human institutions and the committees, coalitions, and networks that form within them, make mistakes, that "God's truth [alone] abideth still" and therefore we need to be a little more modest—all of us—about claiming that our truth is God's truth, and altogether more cautious about asking one another to leave the church, the banquet table to which Jesus Christ himself has invited us.

Finally, the author, out of his own life experience, urges his clerical readers, particularly, to take care of themselves, reminding us that our primary jobs include preaching—read, work, struggle, sweat over it; being an accessible pastor—know them, love them, be available to them; and administration—enable the institution to do what it believes God wants it to do. This wise teacher/pastor tells us that we are not the church's savior, that we are limited as are all people and that unattended personal needs will make us less able to be the ministers we aspire to be. Time off, diet, rest, exercise, reading, time to be with and enjoy our beloveds—sound and necessary advice from one who, I sense, has struggled all his life with the conflicts between professional expectation and personal need.

John Galloway begins this good book with a reference to ministers nearing retirement "looking back in anguish," and wanting somehow to contribute something to healing and revitalizing our practice of ministry in a way that will help all of us one day "look back" with a measure of satisfaction and gratitude. It is, I know, a job quite unlike any other. Daily, ministers are privileged to be part of life's most intimate moments: birth, marriage, illness, crisis, celebration, death. Daily, ministers are privileged to deal with ultimate things and to perform such a variety of duties all the way from seeing that the furnace is working to giving Bibles to third-graders, privileged to live a life that is blessedly busy and full of joyous potential. John Galloway has given his readers a wonderful gift from his own busy, happy, and faithful ministry.

May his readers and his imitators thrive and may their numbers increase!

John M. Buchanan

Acknowledgments

*O*ne of my seminary profs suggested that many people enter the ordained ministry because they like to work alone. There is a good deal of truth to that, but we clergy types all know that we cannot work alone and be in ministry. Ministry is a communal reality.

Certainly it has been so for me, especially in preparing this manuscript. Special thanks are owed to the folks who have prayed for and helped edit and critique my ramblings.

I offer my gratitude first to Mary Jo Meneely, my secretary, who has typed, retyped, and retyped again. I want to thank Janice Anderson, Steven Harberts, Margaret Romeis, and Sally Waterstraat, who have read and edited and offered most helpful corrections and improvements.

Lastly, I want to offer gratitude that defies words to my wife, Susan. Her love, encouragement, and prayers have made ministry possible for me. Her input on this manuscript has been invaluable. She has been diagnosed with Lou Gehrig's Disease (ALS), an illness that has robbed her of her ability to walk and to talk. Her written input and silent prayers sustain me even as these words are written. To her this book is dedicated.

Introduction

If I had a brain in my head, I wouldn't be writing these thoughts just now. Spilling the beans can make a mess. Had wisdom prevailed, I'd have waited until I retired so that I could lay out what it's like to be a pastor these days, without then having to face the congregation I serve, knowing that now they know.

Several factors have come together to drive me to take up the pen and jot down what little wisdom I have, in hopes of being helpful. For one thing I am now old enough that several of my protegés are drawing their pensions in some form of retirement. As they have hung up their vestments for the last time, their words to me have a common ring. In one way or another they rejoice to be out of it. They voice the feeling that now they can begin to live. "I'm getting out just in time," several of them have said.

Since it was common "back in those days" for us to enter seminary right out of college, my cronies have logged their forty years in the pastoral wilderness and now look forward to the promised land. As they toe the banks of their retirement Jordan River, their hearts seem broken. I hear biting words, looking back in anguish at how they feel they were treated. Tears are not uncommon. To hear gifted persons who were called by God and put in their two score years serving the church of Jesus Christ sum it all up in frustration, resentment, and hurt is upsetting to my soul. It makes me wonder what is happening to us in this vocation of ours.

Persons who have left the ordained clergy in midcareer ask me, "How are you able to stay with it?" "Why haven't you quit?" "How do you put up with all the [here various words are used, none of them theological] that goes on every day in the church?"

I ask if they would ever consider going back. Their "No" is quite definite. The ministry, as they remember it, is not something they would ever endure again. Their wounds are deep. Their resentment has become a part of who they are.

Now I learn that, although mainline denominations are shrinking in numbers, we have a clergy shortage. This in no small part is because able young people do not feel themselves called to live the kind of life they see their pastors living. Not that our lives should be all that attractive, mind you. Something about a pastor's life should be hardship. We should have a conspicuous witness of having denied ourselves, of taking up our cross and following Jesus. Ministry is not meant to be a glitzy, high-roller lifestyle in the fast lane. But it is supposed to exude a sense of inner peace that comes from doing the Lord's work. Young people sensing the call of God should see in us that inner spark that comes from our doing the most important work in the world. But too often the spark has been extinguished.

Too many churches have in them what one writer has called "clergy killers." Instead of doing the Lord's work, pastor after pastor has to fight to survive. Even if no "clergy killers" are lurking in the church hallways, too many parishes still make their pastor's life a nightmare. Young people see in too many of us a person who has been beaten down. When the opportunity comes along to serve the Lord quite faithfully in some calling other than the pastorate, young people hear that still small voice roaring like a lion, telling them to serve anywhere they can, other than as pastor of a local congregation.

Is my own Presbyterian denomination typical? Only about half of the master of divinity students at our seminaries are Presbyterian. Of them, only about half intend to enter the pastorate as pastor or associate pastor. Of those that do, once in the parish at least 20 percent will leave within the first five years. And still more will fall away with the passing of time.

Some optimists see hope in the number of second-career people entering our seminaries. They figure that a person who has been "toughened" by the marketplace or the military will be well prepared to withstand the rigors of a congregation. Unfortunately, the environment in which a pastor functions is so diametrically opposed to life in either the marketplace or the military that experience in those places teaches what one might call "bad habits" for ministry. The corporate or military models just don't cut it with the Thursday morning sewing group or the Tuesday morning men's Bible class. My experience has been that few folks can make the transition from corporate/military to pastorate and have a fruitful ministry. Marital crises, emotional disorders, alcohol or drug abuse, and an early exit from ministry are not uncommon for second-career people.

The worst image I have is of the pastor whose marriage is not in jeopardy, whose position as minister of a particular church is under no unusual threat, who does not entertain thoughts of bolting from the cloth to take up a life in some other pursuit, but who died mentally, emotionally, and spiritually several years ago. The poor reverend has simply given up. It just seems to be too late to risk a new life doing anything else. "Besides, who would have me? No hope exists of being called to another congregation. This is what I know and I am afraid to try what I do not know. So I endure." Sad to say, this is the state for far too many among us. They have just given up. The parish has beaten the life out of them. They put up with the occasional outrageous behavior of parishioners because they are afraid to do otherwise. So they and their parish go through hollow motions until the Board of Pensions calls the good reverend home.

The miracle is that, having written all this, I still believe the parish ministry is the only place I would ever want to be. I believe I was called by God to do this and I believe God still wants me to be doing it. Where else do you get in on the ultimate issues every day? No aspect of life is out of bounds for us. I could not imagine dedicating my life to doing anything else. We who are in ministry walk with people through birth, marriage, illness, firings, promotions, despair, and unspeakable joy. We stand with families beside an open grave. We counsel with them as they face critical decisions. The headlines of the newspaper are our world. Where else can you drink in the fullness of life and get paid for it, not all that well, mind you, but more than some of us deserve?

This book is written in the hope of sharing some of the insights that have popped into my skull as I have hung around pastor's homes and studies for sixty years, when you count having lived in my father's parsonage before living in my own preacher's house.

I am thoroughly convinced that though the parish is a minefield, many pastors get themselves into trouble by barging headlong into their own pigheaded foolishness. A few points of wisdom could prevent some of the most outrageous of mistakes. Pastors need a better sense of pacing. We all need a clearer image of what this thing called "congregation" really is. While I firmly believe we cannot ever guarantee that any of us can dodge all the slings and arrows of parish life, and while I also believe some of the best among us have taken more than their share of flack, there is comfort nonetheless in sensing that, regardless of the outcome, we have faithfully and fairly conducted our ministry.

Through it all, we need to regain our courage. If I had but one observation it would be that we have become a bunch of chickens. We hassle and whine and manipulate, often making a big deal of minor issues. We do not seem to have the courage to lead on the issues that matter most. As a group, we in the clergy do not have a compelling sense of vision. We have lost the capacity to dream about what is possible. We have given up on our own ministry and congregation, becoming content with lack of commitment, assuming this is how it is these days. We just find it safer not to dream dreams. We play career games. We lie to one another. We serve on boards. We strut at denominational gatherings. And our churches just stay the same old same old.

This book is written because I hear too many colleagues express a sense of being "over against" the congregation they serve. Us/them language sneaks into conversations when we pastors talk shop. Frustration with parishioners' ineptitude, what the clergy have perceived (often erroneously) to be lack of commitment, legalism, small-mindedness, and a host of other complaints spice up our chats.

A thesis of this book is that a certain "over-againstness" goes with the turf of being a minister. In an effort to explain how we might better understand the particular ways church folks go about whatever it is church folks do, I will offer the model of the congregation as a family reunion. The model gives the comfort of knowing that some "over-againstness" is inevitable and OK. We are not being singled out to be shunned, criticized, or discriminated against. It's just that we are arriving in a situation that has a history and identity of its own, and we need to take time patiently and gently to settle in.

People have their reasons for not knowing what to do with us. There is good reason why we stand in a rather odd relationship to these souls. Understanding why this is and learning to be patient with it, we can lay a foundation for a fruitful, joyous pastorate. We can establish ground on which to stand and from which to lead.

The model is designed to help us appreciate the congregation. I will write in an easygoing, lighthearted style, not because I do not take ministry seriously, but because I believe we can all have joy, even in our serving.

The style of the book will be anecdotal rather than being based on statistical research. Quite frankly I do not relate on a daily basis to 52.7 percent of all persons between the ages of eighteen and twenty-three. I can, however, tell you from firsthand experience about the twenty-two-year-old who was in my study last Thursday. It is in our stories that our ministry takes on life.

I had considered a title that included the words "hint of sanity." I had intended to use the word "sanity" because we need to get past our illusions and denials to face reality. I was going to use the word "hint" because in another sense I don't take sanity too seriously. Yes, I know a number of our colleagues are facing some very serious emotional problems and I do not, in any way, want to be casual about their affliction. I simply wanted to state what is obvious to many folks already. We mainline denominational types tend to be the most boringly sane cast of characters ever gathered in the name of Christ. In fact I believe one of the reasons our denominations have declined is that we are dying of sanity. We are terribly rational. We are programmed. We just don't get funky and say shocking things or take chances or run risks or see a new opportunity and run headlong for it. We do things decently and in order. And, oh my goodness, are we sane!

Did you ever stop to think that the place that most exudes doing it decently and in order is the local cemetery? The people who manage it have their procedures down pat. New members are received in solemn ceremonies. An organizational chart on the office wall explains in detail where all the members stand (OK, lie) in relation to all the other members. There are no conflicts. Nobody ever encroaches on (or under) anyone else's turf. People don't quit and join another cemetery. They are all there in their proper places every Sunday. Everyone knows his or her place and stays in it. It is the most decent and orderly place in town. There just isn't a whole lot of life there.

So another theme of these jottings will be that we need to know where and how to loosen up. We need to know when and how to go for the gusto. We need to think about what few battles need to be fought, and what battles just aren't worth it. We need to regain our courage and our excitement about the parish ministry.

The good news is that we can! Our calling is an exciting place to be. If we patiently understand our parishioners and work with them, there are no more rewarding adventures than being pastor of a local congregation.

So, I hope pastors will be helped by these pages. I hope seminary students and people considering ministry will have triggered within them a heartfelt wrestling with what ministry is and can be. I believe members of a congregation will get a better appreciation of what their pastor faces. Most of all, I hope pastors and small groups of laypersons can read this together, discuss the issues, and come to have a better understanding of each other. I believe members of a local congregation can gain some insights for their ministries, especially as they are joining a new church.

It would help if we all were more patient and at the same time more creatively visionary—not an easy art, by any means. We will flesh it out in the chapters to come. For now prepare to read, holding the thought that we are not meant to be strangers doing battle in our churches. We are meant to be the family of God.

When we get to know the people in our congregation, to love them, to be with them for a time, we ourselves begin in wonderful ways to be part of their very special family.

Life has few greater joys.

Part I   Coming to Town

Chapter 1

Family Reunion

*L*et's imagine we are driving onto the grounds of the mythical Four Leaf Clover Hotel and Convention Center. In addition to signs directing us where to park, where to register, where to find the Clover Dining Room adjacent to the Clover Lounge featuring a happy hour and Karaoke Night, we cannot miss the big portable marquee welcoming the ACME Heating Company, the Gutter Ball Bowlers, and the Smythe Family Reunion.

Out on the rolling, well-kept grounds we spot our destination: a large tent fronted by a "Smythe Family Reunion" banner flapping in the wind. People of all ages clustered around the tent would appear to be a gaggle of Smythes.

We check in at the front desk before going to the reunion. Several official-, dare I say officious-looking people mill around wearing laminated "Smythe Family Reunion" name tags. Apparently they are the welcoming committee. They have been expecting us, and they recognize us instantly. Bud and Loretta Smythe greet us, welcome us with broad smiles, and remind us:"Remember, we are not Smiths. Smiths are different from us. We are Smythes and proud of it."

We have just arrived as the newly called "Facilitator of Smythe Family Reunions." Some Smythes will tear up at how wonderful it is that the Lord has brought us to be their facilitator. They will claim to love us and want to support us.

"You are in our prayers, Facilitator." "Anything we can do to help, you can count on us." But they will break our hearts when we overhear them telling anyone who will listen that we can't possibly do nearly as well as the last facilitator did, before leaving for the bigger and more challenging Jackson family reunions. Still others, who had a bad experience with our predecessor, will make us uneasy by announcing that they are going to watch us closely to see if we are "the same kind." That will come later. Now, at first blush, all is rosy. Bud and Loretta and the people we meet under the tent welcome us with open arms. All is well in the kingdom.

While at no time did we ever define with the Smythes exactly what a facilitator is expected to do, we all seem to have a general understanding. We just
do what facilitators do. Besides, we were the Associate Facilitator at the Grant
family reunions for the last three years, and prior to that we were in school
taking courses on the history of hotels and general weather conditions in New
England. This had little to do with actually dealing with Smythes on a day-to-
day basis, but it made us think we knew our stuff and conferred on us a certain status that made Bud and Loretta welcome us with more than a modicum
of respect.

As we will no doubt discover in our first fifteen minutes glad-handing under
the tent, each family possesses its own personality, its own history, its own
touchy points, its own well-established ways of being family and running
reunions. The Smythes have been at it for years, and their habits are set in
stone. So we are arriving to pick up the ongoing enterprise of people we really
do not know, in a facility we do not recognize, to lead them at a reunion whose
activities they have already been practicing for years quite well without us,
thank you, with well-cultivated idiosyncrasies we have never seen in our lives.
In an assignment that might be called "mission impossible," they look to us to
lead. To complicate our assignment, they will for a period of time accept our
leadership, but only insofar as it reinforces the Smythe way of doing things, a
way they refuse to make clear to us until we violate it and incur their scorn.

As we let the absurdity of that image marinate in our minds, let me suggest
that in all my years of ministry, this is the best image I know to describe what
it is like to arrive on the scene as the "new pastor" of our "new flock." We are
the facilitators at an extended family reunion in a family to which we do not
belong, who have a well-developed style we have never seen, in a place we
do not recognize.

Dream with me on this one. Aunt Bessie always brings potato salad. Her
eyes are going bad and she is getting forgetful, and rumor has it Cousin Irene
had indigestion last year after wolfing down two helpings of Auntie's finest.
But everybody loves Bessie. They know it would break her precious heart not
to be able to bring that potato salad or to see any of it go uneaten.

Our immediate temptation is to rescue the situation by saving the Smythes
from food poisoning. After all, we had a fieldwork assignment where the
people made delicious potato salad and passed on the recipe to us. We could
stop the indigestion, improve the cuisine, and make the reunion better. We
could ease Bessie away from making potato salad and have her set the tables.
It sounds simple.

But we dare not try! Wisdom says, "Leave it alone." Only a fool of a facilitator would try to improve the situation by challenging Bessie. The Smythes

already know the drawbacks of Aunt Bessie's cooking, and they have learned to cope with it in their own way, even if it means hiding the potato salad one forkful at a time in the garbage. The fact that better potato salad could be served is not the issue. That the threat of tummyaches could be lessened is not the issue. The issue here is family.

Then there is Uncle Fred. Uncle Fred has a game he used to play as a boy on the farm, when life was slower and folks were evidently desperate for anything that would pass the time of day. For the past forty-seven years Uncle Fred has had enough clout in the family to get all the youngsters to play his game. It is a tradition now. Moms and dads gather to watch their children do what they themselves did, not so many years back – play Uncle Fred's game. Of course the kids hate it. That is, except Wilbur and Debbie's little girl, who wins at everything, including boring games. Three of the boys sneak away, two children cry and several of the more assertively trained protest loudly, exclaiming this is the last stupid reunion they ever plan to attend.

This is a unique opportunity, a dull-witted facilitator thinks, to rescue the children and preserve the interest of future generations in attending Smythe reunions. The mentally challenged among us believe it is time to take over from Uncle Fred so that a more relevant, more child-friendly game can be played; the kind we read about a few months back in *Facilitator's Journal*. If we believe that, we are doomed.

All we need to do is suggest that we put Uncle Fred and his game out to pasture, and the moms and dads will run us out of town before the sun goes down. "We played that game when we were kids. So what if the kids hate it? We did too. But that's part of who we are. Who are you to butt in anyway? Besides, we need to thank Fred for his years of service." It does not matter if at our former assignment we had the best children's game program in the Western world. At the Smythe reunion, Uncle Fred's games are a mainstay.

You get the drift. It is a family with a history. Before we ever think of changing it, or worse yet "rescuing" it, we need to learn to appreciate what it is and how it functions.

The image of a family reunion swept over me one night years ago at a gala event hosted by someone in the church I then served. The guest list included a high percentage of parishioners. After dinner and a short program we were treated to slides and super 8 movies from yesteryear, a collection from the school days era, in this case the prep school era. I was caught off guard by the way most of the guests jumped into the action. "Hey, look, there's you, Charlie! Who's that girl with you?" "Laura, you haven't changed a bit." "Oh, look at me. And who . . . good grief that's you, Sally! There you are, Tom." They all knew each other from this former era, an era in which I had not participated.

Though by then I had come to feel that I had a close friendship with practically everyone in the room, it was obvious that they had a lifelong bond I could never share. Even after almost a decade with them, I suddenly realized that they were like family in a way I was not. For all my years with these people, I was still something of an outsider, a newcomer.

Congregations are families. Even in highly mobile communities, the pastor arrives at a church where the core of members already have a history of experience that the pastor does not share. Just like families, they have a history of spats, conquests, griefs, weddings, harrowing moments, recollections of support and friendship, a feeling of being at home with one another. In fact, in smaller rural churches many of the people actually are blood relatives. Look around the building of any congregation founded more than a generation ago and it will give the feel of walking into a family's homestead or the family room of a suburban colonial. Pictures hang on the wall of former family leaders. Black-and-white shots show youth groups, Sunday school classes, groundbreaking ceremonies, times the church family let down its hair at a special occasion. Picture directories can be found, family albums really. Plaques remind us of the family members who pitched in to help pay for refurbishing a room or to buy an article of furniture.

A discerning eye watching the church family interact will note that they might have a written constitution, but the real authority in the place is informal, vested in persons who have earned respect over the years. When the family gathers for devotions, they follow a liturgy that roughly approximates that of many other families in their denomination. But they have developed certain sacred wrinkles unique to them. We soon learn that expert knowledge of liturgy does not in any way give us permission to brush aside those sacred wrinkles, for many of them are sacred indeed. Family members love certain songs and just don't cotton to others. They don't have assigned seats. It's just that over the years some of them have come to realize they worship best when seated in a particular spot.

Listen to them and they'll share their memories: the time there was a fire in one of the classrooms; the benefit supper to raise money when Clyde had his accident; the way the ladies worked all night thirty years ago to put on the big dinner in October when the caterer backed out at the last minute; the time Pastor Allen lost his glasses and could not read his sermon. And of course, although they don't like to talk about it (though everybody does), the scandal when Dr. Misbrow ran off with the oldest O'Neill sister. Yep. It's a family all right.

Called on to facilitate an ongoing family reunion, we just need to remember: They are family; we are not. It does not matter how much we know. It does not matter how good we are. It does not matter if we attended a lecture that proved our way of doing it is right and their way of doing it is wrong. They are family; we are not. They have a long history with each other; we have just shown up.

If we have an IQ over 80, we know not to walk in and try to take over. We know the only wise course of action is getting to know the Smythes. Spend time milling around under the tent, listening, hearing stories. Hear their pain and their adamant resolve not to be Smiths and their belligerence toward anyone who confuses them with Smiths. Find out who has respect among them, who really sits at the head of the table. Meet the various personalities. Who likes whom? Who has a grudge against whom? What is it Smythes do at a reunion anyway, and how do they do it? How do they plan and decide? What are their dreams and what are their fears?

Then gradually, in a nonintrusive way, we can try to help them celebrate. That's the point after all. Make those people who came to the Four Leaf Clover Hotel and Convention Center to attend the heating company or bowling league conventions wish they were Smythes. Help the family show their love for each other. Help them rejoice to be Smythes, to share in thanksgiving for the times they share together, and to praise the Lord who made them family.

As we will see, there are ways over time we will settle in and have our impact. Gradually we will be embraced and made to feel at home. We will even garner authority. At the beginning, remember they are family. It is their reunion and we've only just arrived to facilitate.

Chapter 2

Do Nothing

At the risk of damaging our ministerial pride, it must be said that quite often churches find their most creative moments come when they have no full-time pastor. The period between the time when one minister leaves and another arrives can be enormously invigorating for local congregations. Members who grieve the departure of the former pastor sometimes work extra hard to see that the legacy of our dearly departed and still much beloved reverend is carried on in a manner befitting such a wonderful pastorate. Those who are glad that the louse has finally left town see the interim period as a chance to prepare the way for a brighter future. Those who have no real opinion about our now ex-preacher realize everyone has to pitch in just to keep the church going. The congregation awakens to its own dependence on one another. People work together with a sense of hope that perhaps, against all odds, the search committee will actually find the perfect minister who will have all the former pastor's strengths and none of the former pastor's weaknesses, a person who will challenge everyone without offending anyone. Anticipation hangs in the air.

By the very act of showing up, we ministers run the risk of ruining all the anticipation. The trick is to show up and not mess up—a delicate art that is best carried out when we discipline ourselves to realize, first, that the church was doing quite well before we got there. Second, we are a greater threat to destroy the church's spirit than we are to generate it. Despite all our best efforts and intentions, the church sees our arrival as reason for a sigh of relief. "Now that the new minister is here, we can take it easy. Let the new minister do it. We will do less." As we unpack our boxes of books to arrange each volume neatly on the proper shelf in the pastor's study, we have already signaled to the congregation a message to recede into the background, to cheer us on as we do ministry for them.

In this chapter we explore the issue of how to cope with a congregation's desire to let the reverend do it. The answer is compassionate, focused laziness. Just don't do much.

My late father, who was himself a pastor, gave me a rule to live by in ministry. "Don't do anything new in your first year." While no rule can be absolute, this one is pretty good. I have not yet seen a ministry get into trouble because this rule was followed, though I have seen many pastorates pushed headlong into troubled waters because the rule was violated.

Just ponder for a moment what a relief it is to know that for one year we do not have to remake the church! What a weight has been lifted from our shoulders to know that we have a yearlong reprieve!

Relax! Let's put our feet up, kick back, let everyone know that the church has survived the interim because people pitched in, prayed, and pulled together. Now even though such a wonderfully gifted pastor (they think that when we are new) has appeared on the scene, the church still can survive only if people continue to pitch in, pray, and pull together. Our arrival does not change a thing. We are still the family of faith, the church of Jesus Christ, dependent on the Spirit moving among us as we each express our gifts for the common good.

What an opportunity that first year can be! Before we have to come up with new ideas, we have time to read all the minutes of all the governing boards and committees of the church for the past five years. Quit laughing—I'm not joking. Admittedly, these documents do not read like a best-selling novel, but they are about the people we are getting to know in a place with which we are growing familiar. We will find them surprisingly interesting. They have plot lines. We can see the points where issues became divisive. We can spot the frustrated efforts of repeatedly trying to do something that has not happened, something that has been brought up at every other meeting for the last five years, and still no one has taken action on it. We can see who are the doers and who are the stoppers. We can rejoice that the church has done some good things. We can be warned what not to recommend because the church has a sour taste in its mouth about it. They tried it and hated it. We have our eyes opened as to how this family of faith carries on its life together. We have a year to listen and learn before opening our big mouths.

Instead of drafting elaborate memos to urge the church to restructure its organization, we have time to understand and appreciate the organization as it already exists. We have a once-in-a-ministry opportunity to do some major reconnaissance work. We can see what the organizational chart looks like on paper and, more importantly, we have time to learn what the informal organization really is. We can come to know where the power is actually lodged, who has the leverage, whose voice is heard and why.

One of the rude awakenings that will inevitably come to us, as we take time to study the congregation, is that the organizational model in this and in every church has been turned somewhat on its ear because the church has in its membership "certain individuals." Need I say more? Over time certain highly dedicated and usually quite competent persons have given so much of their time to a certain area of the church's life that the committee or board that ought to have had authority in that area has simply abdicated to these individuals who now have unchecked power. Alas, these individuals usually happen to be of a personality type that does not work well in committee. So we have loose cannons controlling quite large areas of the church's life. We cannot carry on effectively until we know who these persons are, how they function, how well their efforts express the actual will of the congregation. The good news is that our call just now is not to worry about such individuals. After all, it is only the first year. Our present task is only to learn what is happening. We can evaluate it later. We can think about changing it later still.

We have a year to practice with the church a polity whereby committees report to the ruling board, which then makes the final decisions. Surprisingly, most leaders in the congregation actually do want to know how a church is supposed to function. They are really quite teachable. We can rehearse the fact that the clergy do not run the church. They'll like that. We have a constitution that distributes power quite clearly and quite effectively. We can take our time to learn how together we can make the constitution work.

We have time to learn how the church bulletin is put together, how the order of worship flows. Unless the worship committee and the church's ruling body are vocally unhappy with that order of worship, we have no need to try to change it—at least not yet. We have a year to worship God with our new church family as they have always done it.

We can move at a leisurely pace to discern what the real lines of communication are. What are the groupings in the church, and who are the influential people in each of these clusters? If we wanted to get a message out, who would we tell? Who would have to be informed? How would the word flow through the church? Who reads the newsletter? Who puts the newsletter together?

In that first year we want to give all the help we can to the poor soul who recruits Sunday school teachers.

Then there is the poor character who drew the short straw and has to run this year's stewardship campaign.

The music program needs to be thanked and affirmed.

The women's and men's organizations need our pastoral support and a gentle affirming nod.

The first year is an opportunity to be in touch with persons who have visited the church to see if they might like to become members. There is nothing like sizable new-member classes to rejuvenate a sense of hope within the congregation.

Obviously, this first year of doing nothing takes a lot of work. It is productive work because it focuses our energy. What energy we do exert is to help already existing groups. We are largely relaxed and at ease about it because we are not at all like Sisyphus in the myth, endlessly rolling a heavy stone up a hill. We are not rolling stones at all. We are relaxing. If we want to pitch in, we can pitch in to move chairs and help set up tables according to the appropriate committee's or individual's desired arrangement. We can help them do it the way they have always done it. We have come to be their servant, not their supervisor. We exert no energy trying to change them.

And get this: We celebrate when they tell us, "We've always done it this way." Yes, you read it correctly. We celebrate when they tell us, "We've always done it this way." We celebrate because how else would we know how they've always done it, and how else would we ever be able to help them evaluate what it is that they do?

You know the best part? Not one of the church's flaws is our fault. Any criticism we hear is voiced about what was set up before we got here. We can hear complaints about the church without feeling the least bit threatened. It's wonderful. We should be slow to ruin it.

We have a honeymoon when we can sort through which battles need to be fought and which do not. We can see what should be changed and what should not. What we might initially have thought was not a very effective part of this church's ministry, we might in time discover is surprisingly effective and vital to the organization's life together. In fact, that very ministry we had thought was useless turns out to be the centerpiece of that congregation's rightful identity. What we might have thought made no theological sense may prove to have great theological integrity after all. We become aware where the momentum for God's work already exists within the family.

We cannot emphasize this point enough. God is already at work. The church already has a hunger to grow spiritually, to worship God, to serve God by serving others. We just need some time to discern the specifics of this hunger. Disciplining ourselves not to jump in and remake the church will prove to be our only way to understand the uniqueness of this church's mission in the world.

It is indeed a blow to our pride as movers and shakers to realize that the more we try to do in our first year, the less effective we are. Instead of seeing ourselves as agents to change the institution, we serve best by seeing ourselves as human beings who at the end of the first year should have instilled a marvelous feeling of trust within the congregation. "This minister understands us." "This minister affirms us." "This minister has helped us celebrate that we are God's family." "Now, by God's Spirit working through us, good things are going to happen here."

Chapter 3

It's Not My Church

About thirty of us sat in the church parlor one Saturday morning discussing different ways ministers around the country were shepherding their respective flocks through whatever were their conflicts du jour. It was good conversation, led by a former professor of mine from seminary days. I opted to jump into the fray by saying something to the effect that "I don't know how other ministers lead their congregation, but in my church we do thus and such." Our guest speaker was quick to say, "John, if you think it's *your* church, the congregation is in trouble." A very gracious as well as brilliant person, he quickly added in front of "my" parishioners that he knew he could say such a thing because he knew I was able to take it. He thus also reminded me that take it I must.

For all the chuckles that followed our little interplay, the man had a profound point. If I think it is "my" church, trouble is crouching at the door.

I won't absolutize. There is nothing wrong with a person saying to a friend who is searching for a church home, "Let me take you to *my* church this Sunday." A pastor may legitimately drive a newcomer through the neighborhood and say, "There's the school. There's the post office. And there, coming into view, is *my* church." Our weekend guest speaker was not suggesting we pass a rule that none of us ever say "my" church or "our" church.

What he meant was that no pastor ought ever to use the word "my" to imply "I own it," or to say, "It is mine to do with as I please." Our speaker was using a quick verbal jab to remind me that this congregation is not my possession, and therefore I do not have control over it. He was thinking of "my" in the sense; "This is *my* room. I'll decorate it any way I want." "It is *my* money. I'll spend it as I please." "It is *my* hair. I can wear it in any style I desire."

Picture the reaction if we swagger into the Smythe family reunion and tell them, "This is my reunion." My hunch is they would wonder what we are talking about. They might grant us that it is "our" assignment to be "their" facilitator. "But, pastor, this just is not 'your' reunion."

The surest way to ruin a ministry is to figure: "This is *my* church. I will do exactly what I want because I am in charge around here. I've got the power; they'd better cower." It is the kiss of death.

Odd as it may sound, the defining moments that have solidified my ministry in each of my last three churches were moments when I had no control at all. They were moments I felt no power. Indeed, one could say that each congregation became "my" church family in the best sense of the term at precisely the instant when matters were spinning out of "my" control.

A community action group had been invited by yours truly to use an office in our building. I served on the group's board. As a result of some less than tactful activities by this group, many folks in town became convinced we were all a bunch of Communists. One lady in our church became so enraged at the "subversive" threat that she informed me in no uncertain terms that she was not going to take it any more. She was giving up Russian dressing in protest of our Communist activities. Another parishioner told me this was the worst crisis the church had faced since the preacher's wife got into a fistfight with the president of the women's association at a church supper back in the late 1800s, a fight that was not halted until one of the combatants drew a hat pin and threatened to use it. Mine was obviously a serious crisis to be in league with that.

The monthly meeting of our ruling board was coming up. Whether to let the group stay in the building was on the agenda. There were no absences that night. Everyone was there, and everyone was ready. The debate was insightful, civil, determined, and very serious. Unfortunately, some of the argument centered on the need to support the pastor, to show trust, not to embarrass me. I was clearly linked to the cause of keeping the group in the building. This was, after all, John's group.

When the votes were counted, our ruling body had ruled by one vote that the group had to go. I had lost. My side had been defeated. The group on whose board I served was being tossed out. Since the ruling board had openly discussed this as "my" project, I had to wonder if maybe the church's leaders were sending me a message.

The next morning I came into the office deflated. I wondered if I were still wanted. Around 9:30 I heard the voice of a board member at the secretary's desk just outside my door. It was the voice of someone who had voted to throw the group out. I heard the voice ask what sounded like a silly question, no reason to justify coming all the way downtown to ask it in person. Then I heard her say, "Is John in?" "Yes. He's in his office." In the frame of my open door appeared the board member. "Hey, John. I was just in the office and thought I'd stop by and say 'hi.'" With that she was gone.

Half an hour later I heard the voice of another negative voter. "Is John in?" In the open door stood the silhouette of a board member who had never before come into the building at this time of day. "Hey, John, just wanted to see how you're doing. Don't take last night too hard. Hang in there, man." With that he vanished.

Ten minutes later another one popped into the doorframe. "John, I don't think I tell you often enough how much I appreciate what you are doing. Our whole family loves you. Keep up the good work."

Investigation revealed they had not talked to each other. They each individually wanted to come in just to see how I was doing. They sensed I had been hurt, and that hurt them. They did not want to lose me. They wanted to comfort me and help me back to my feet so we could all go on together. In my weakness and defeat, I found their love, and with that my ministry began in that place.

A decade later I was serving another church. Late one Saturday night my sister called to say that our father had had a stroke and was quite ill in a New Jersey hospital. My father used to tell my sister and me that he was convinced we had it in for him because, if either of us ever had to be taken to the emergency room, it was always Saturday night, when he needed a good night's rest before the rigors of Sunday morning. That night it felt like payback time.

I made the decision to tough it out at church the next morning. I reasoned that if I told no one about my father's illness, I could make it through the morning without having to face my own emotions. The first service went without a hitch. The strategy was working. The class I taught between services was no problem. In fact there were lots of laughs. I'm going to make it, I thought. Then I made a fateful error. Fifteen minutes into our second service, I thought that perhaps I should tell the congregation just before the benediction. I would solicit their prayers. That was a stupid thing to think, because the very thought of telling them opened up in me the very emotions that I knew I would feel when I actually told them. I frantically tried to suppress the thought, which stubbornly kept popping up every two seconds.

Just before the sermon the congregation sang a hymn which, wouldn't you know it, was "Be Still, My Soul," the great hymn to the tune "Finlandia." That had been the anthem the choir had sung at a special retirement celebration for my father a decade before, a service I had attended and whose memory now consumed my thoughts. During the first stanza I realized, This is going to be tough—this hymn might do me in. If you are familiar with the hymn, you know that each stanza goes on for some time. All during that first stanza I was fading. During the second stanza I was done in. Fortunately, my chair was right by the door, and I left the chancel to become a blubbering idiot out of everyone's sight. For the first time in my ministry, I actually hoped the hymn before the sermon would have thirty-seven stanzas. Alas, it did not, and though each stanza took its full time, the hymn ended before I had pulled myself together.

The congregation sat and gazed at the pulpit, expecting someone in a robe to pop up and preach. Patiently they waited. Tension gripped my fellow liturgists and the choir. After a time I went back into the sanctuary, mounted the pulpit steps, and looked out at the congregation, who could see I was a mess. Only then did I realize I could not utter a word. They looked at me; I looked at my notes.

Now when we serve as pastor of a church, we expect to be in charge, in control, on top of every situation. Our sermons are prepared and delivered with polish. Like the character in Tom Wolfe's novel, *Bonfire of the Vanities,* we are the "Master of the Universe." This is "our" church and we are in command.

Not that day. After what seemed an eternity, I choked out a few words about my father's stroke, and said something about his injunction that the preacher must always act like a pro. Then I mumbled through a message with a handkerchief in one hand and a glass of water in the other. It was about as humiliating an experience as I have ever had. I had no control of my own emotions, and five hundred parishioners, including members of my family, got to watch.

An odd thing happened that morning. It has been said that in worship an audience is supposed to become a congregation. That morning we went a step beyond. For a time the congregation became family. For years after that day people spoke lovingly of having been there. I am convinced that at least two hundred more people than were there still recall it vividly. My humiliation was the occasion of my inclusion. It was a moment of being embraced, a moment that let my ministry really begin.

One would think that I would have learned the lesson well enough by these two experiences. Evidently, the Lord felt I needed to learn more. Not long after arriving at the church I'm serving as I write this, an annual physical revealed that my PSA count had gone up slightly. A follow-up blood test three months later revealed that it had gone up farther. An appointment scheduled with a urologist led to a biopsy, and within days the report came back that I had prostate cancer. "Lord, isn't there some way to be received into a church family without all this?" I immediately told the church, and they stepped up to the challenge. When the congregation gathered around me for the laying on of hands and praying for healing at a special prayer service, it was like being transported to a place in our childhood where our family surrounds us, and all is secure. To a great extent, the cancer diagnosis and subsequent surgery were ways in which the congregation discovered itself as a praying family and discovered me as a part of who they are.

The lesson has been drummed into me. It is never "my" church in the sense that I can control it. Indeed, in God's perplexing strategy I cannot serve it until I've lost control. Then, and only then, to my utter amazement the congregation actually begins to become "my" church family.

Chapter 4

Have Patience

*I*n the late fall of 1993 I returned to the community in which I had grown up. Now that I am back, I note that I am involved in several projects that had been initiated long ago, but never brought to completion. For example, we have just finished a building campaign that saw us build a structure connecting what had been two separate buildings. We dedicated our new facility in the fall of 1998. To show the pace at which churches move, we have hanging in our church office an architect's rendering of what this connector might look like. It is a wonderful framed picture, *drawn in 1950!* Almost half a century went by between the time the dream was put on paper and the day we dedicated the actual building.

The Scriptures tell us that a thousand years in God's sight are but as yesterday when it is past. Anyone who has hung around churches for very long knows that it surely feels as though it takes a thousand years to do a day's work. In this marvelous institution run by committees of church people, we readily prove to be footnotes for the wisdom that committees work for hours to put into minutes what should be done in seconds. Churches move at a snail's pace when they move at all.

A friend of mine had been in the ministry for a few years before opting for a career in industry. Then after a few decades in "the real world," he came back into the pastorate. He often said that the biggest difference between working in industry and serving a church is the pace. In church it takes so much longer to do what can be done quite quickly in a business environment. If one wants to serve as pastor of a church, one not only needs to know the truth of my friend's insight; one needs to understand it and to embrace it. Pace is an issue.

The subject is complex because different people inevitably move at different paces. High-powered type A personalities are brought to the edge of a nervous breakdown when we put them on committees. One meeting and they resign. "I can't take it. Nothing happened. It was a waste of time." I recall a board meeting where the president of a local institution was seated next to the wife of a farmer. The executive was frantically motioning me to speed up the proceedings. He often made noises of disgust. His words were always curt and to the point. I was trying to accommodate his wishes and move matters along when the farmer's wife suddenly stopped the meeting to protest that everything was just going too fast. "These are important matters and we need to take the time to hear everyone's thoughts and to listen for the Lord's will. Why is everyone so rush, rush, rush around here?" She had a point. Our job as pastors is to enable these two people to work happily together in the same meeting at the same time. And folks wonder why we feel stress!

Fortunately, people tend to settle into niches that suit their tempo. Trustees, building committee people, and stewardship types like short meetings. The brief memo. The action plan. The tight agenda. I remember one building committee that was chaired by a man who really felt he had no need for much help, and his small committee was quite comfortable with his style. When I first arrived as pastor of the church, I went to his evening meeting scheduled for 7:30. Held up by a matter involving one of my kids, I did not enter the church building until 7:35. As I came to the door where the meeting was to take place, I heard the chairman say, "Amen." I was embarrassed, thinking that I had missed the opening prayer, wondering if the chair had intended for me to be the one who would offer the invocation. My embarrassment turned to mortification and no small amount of surprise when I realized that the "Amen" was at the end of the benediction. The meeting had been adjourned and everyone rose to go home. "Five minutes and we're outta here."

On the other hand, my first meeting with a board of deacons in yet another church was also to convene at 7:30, in someone's living room. Coffee and cookies were served. We sat and enjoyed leisurely conversation. I figured they wanted to get to know me, an idea that quickly left my mind as I noted that no one seemed to care that I was in the room. At 8:15 I was beginning to wonder when we were going to start the meeting. They were busy talking about a couple in the church who were having marital problems. I was not sure about the wisdom of airing what sounded to me more like gossip than anything else. Everyone seemed very comfortable with the conversation. They acted as if it was their Christian duty to carry on this way. They then moved to the subject of a young man in the hospital. Nine o'clock came, and still there had been no call to order, no approval of minutes, no sign that minutes were being taken. Then around 9:30 somebody offered to pray. The prayer mentioned the names that had been chatted about during the course of the evening, and with that everyone got up to go home. I was floored. I guess I am enough of a type

A to think something of a business nature ought to happen at a meeting. How can you have a meeting without calling it to order, having an agenda, making motions, and voting on stuff? I sure was off base that night. To confuse me further, everyone commented how good it was to have me there, and what a wonderful meeting it had been.

By and large it is people with a personality type that is content just to be together, to process (in churches that is a verb) and mull over matters, to chew the fat with little concern about results, who populate our pastoral, fellowship, and mission committees. To the everlasting horror of action-oriented folk, the wheels of most churches grind usually to the pace of "process" people.

Another part of the problem, of course, is that the system itself is slow. Whereas in industry the work force is generally in the office every day, working all day on a problem until it is solved; in churches, a committee is scheduled to meet once a month of an evening. Fifteen people serve on the committee. Only eight show up one particular month, and make a few decisions. A month later nine people attend. Of those, four were in attendance at last month's meeting, though they cannot remember exactly what it was they decided. Five were not there the month before and cannot figure out for the life of them why the minutes record that such idiotic decisions were made. The committee starts from scratch the second month, with a layer of resentment. And so it goes month after month.

Any pastor will be a candidate for the funny farm who actually thinks the church can come to decisions and make major changes quickly. I often hear from pastors who have become emotional basket cases because they thought, If I preach a series of sermons on this issue, everyone will get on board. Or, We'll take this up in our adult education class, and that will change attitudes. Or, I am sending out peacemaking materials. We'll have a class on it and then everyone will begin to sign up to work for peace. To their complete surprise, the sermons, the classes, the materials bear no visible fruits. Before long these pastors begin to feel that they are trying to dig a trench across a lake. Their labors seem to produce virtually no results.

We need to remember that we are facilitating the Smythe family reunion. They had been meeting for a hundred seventy-five years before we arrived, and they plan to be at it for decades, if not centuries, after we are gone, thank you very much.

We draw wisdom from one of the greatest strategists for the local church: Sir Isaac Newton. It was he who (I am convinced he must have just preached his first sermon and moderated his first church board meeting) coined the wisdom that "for every action there is an equal and opposite reaction." That is to say, if we push the congregation in a particular direction, their natural instinct is to push back in the opposite direction. The harder we push, the harder they push. Alas we fail to achieve a Charles Atlas kind of dynamic tension, which should strengthen the body. Instead we weaken the body and produce a fellowship whose momentum is going in exactly the wrong direction.

Two passages of Scripture offer helpful insight. In James 5:7b-8a we read: "The farmer waits for the precious crop from the earth, being patient with it until it receives the early and the late rains. You also must be patient." Paul writes to the Corinthians, "I planted, Apollos watered, but God gave the growth. So neither the one who plants nor the one who waters is anything, but only God who gives the growth" (1 Cor. 3:6–7).

I take great comfort in these words. They tell me it is not up to me to prove *now* that I am an effective pastor. I do not need immediate signs of progress. I merely do my part, knowing that the greatest fruit of my ministry may not be seen in my lifetime. It is for me to trust the Lord, who is very able to move through me and through the church at the Lord's pace, the Lord in whose eyes one day and a thousand years are not dissimilar.

The point is that the Smythe family has to own its own mission. They will not latch onto something because we preach it, or send a memo on it, or get a task force to vote for it, or teach a class on it. They will do it when they are ready. When they do get around to it, it may not come out in a form we had anticipated. We need to give them room to discover, to experience, to stumble onto, to have their own "aha" moment. This takes time. It may not come for a long, long time, and that is OK. It may not come during the time of our pastorate. That is OK too. The Spirit will move among them according to the Spirit's timetable. Ours is not to demand instant results or verification. Ours is to be faithful.

Another insight from these passages is our need for help, if God's work is to be done in God's time. Paul planted. Then he needed Apollos to water. Paul had to swallow his pride. He had to admit that what took place in the Corinthian congregation was not exclusively the result of his brilliant preaching or uncanny knack for church administration. In fact, we get quite the opposite impression from his writing.

Paul knew what we need to know. (1) It is amazing what will happen of lasting value if we let God set the timing. (2) It is amazing what can be done if we don't care who gets the credit. Is it possible that we actually throw off God's timing by trying to maneuver a situation to look like *our* work? Is it possible that God's will is best accomplished in God's time when we are not in a position to get credit?

I recall writing a memo to a committee a few decades ago. I think it was the mission committee. The memo was followed up by a personal presentation by yours truly. If I do say so myself, both the memo and my presentation were quite compelling. At least I was impressed. Unfortunately, neither of my efforts had any impact on the committee. They went on about their business as if my idea had never been voiced. Six months later I made the same suggestion in a committee discussion. About every six months for four years I proposed the idea in one way or another. Nothing. Nada. No impact.

Then one night one of our associate pastors joined the meeting, to answer questions about a project where he had background knowledge. For some reason, after his interrogation ended he lingered with us for a time before making his exit. As the chairperson moved us into discussion of the next item on the agenda, the associate said, "It sounds to me as if you ought to consider . . ." He then spelled out *my* idea to the committee, without having any idea I had been beating my head against a stone wall for four years on that very issue. I was stunned when I heard the chair say, "I like that." A committee member said, "That is exactly the kind of idea we need." Someone else chimed in with, "Why haven't we thought of that before?" The associate was eulogized for *his* insight and *his* fantastic idea.

I wanted to stand up and shout, "Over here, people. Look over here! I've been saying the same thing for the last four years. It's my idea. I thought of it. I presented it. I had the idea first." I didn't do that. In fact I congratulated him on *his* ideas, while thanking God that the committee finally heard it. We went full steam ahead, and the idea became a significant part of our church's life.

In retrospect, we could say that my efforts cultivated the soil, planted the seed, started it all. Had it not been for the work I did, the committee would not have been ready to hear someone else bring the idea. I am not sure we even need to say that, except to comfort my ego, which I confess took a hit that night. Far better to say that in God's scheduling, the time was right and someone other than your author was the right person to speak.

It is amazing what can be done if we do not worry about getting credit, and if we realize God's timing is the only timing that bears fruit.

I am a mediocre golfer. What little I have learned about the game boils down to this. When I try to rush my swing, my game falls apart. A pro golfer once said that when the pressure is on, swing easy. That is good advice for the parish. We need to slow it down. That may seem odd when "nothing seems to be happening around here anyway." When we look objectively at why nothing happens, we may discover that the reason is that the pastor is rushing her or his swing. Our rushing has caused the people to dig in their heels. Swing easy. Be patient. Trust is built slowly. Insight comes slowly. Groups move at their own pace. The Lord is working in this church, and the Lord has a pace for it. More ministries are destroyed because the pastor rushed it than because the pastor faithfully led and left the pace up to the Lord.

With this we end our chapters on arriving. We have tried to drive home the need for humility, patient listening, and appreciating the family that is already there. We have been called to serve these people. If we take a year to do our background homework, we are more likely to be positioned to lead, for, as we are soon to see, passivity is not our final word.

II   Convictions That Drive Us

Chapter 5

Vision

*T*o say that a congregation is like a family reunion is not to say that a congregation should learn how family reunions are run and then try in all ways to do the same thing. There are both subtle and significant points of difference. A reunion is a getting together, a reminiscing, a chance to reconnect and see familiar faces. Being together is the point. Even if activities have been planned for different venues, being together with family in those venues is what matters.

Churches too are filled with folks who figure that's about all we need to do. Let's just be together. Especially in an age when technology isolates us from one another, there is a real hankering just to have fellowship. Who would argue against the family of God gathering together to act in remembrance of our Lord? When Jesus gave advice to the disciples on how to prepare themselves to receive the Holy Spirit, he basically told them to hang out together in one place, pray, and wait. The style of a family reunion has a proper role to play in the life of a local church family.

The trick is to help that church family step beyond the reunion mentality to a more complete expression of the Lord's work. For example, family reunions are not called to attract new people to the fellowship. In fact their purpose is just the opposite. Joneses and Johnsons need not plan to attend the Smythe family reunion. Joneses and Johnsons are not invited. They don't belong. Smythes do all they can to offer a good time for Smythes, and Smythes alone.

A family reunion can be a family reunion without having justice as one of its priorities. Standing against racism, sexism, homophobia, exploitation of the poor are just not issues reunion planners must face. Pooling resources to help fund family reunions in the third world or in the heart of America's inner cities is not on the agenda.

Having a living relationship with a being beyond the family is not why they are together. Though Uncle Caleb will insist that everyone bow while he intones a prayer using words like "vouchsafe" and "limitless bounty," the reunion can be a perfectly fine reunion with a totally secular ambiance. Being people who are twigs on the same family tree and who don't mind making fools of themselves by wearing "Smythe Family Reunion" T-shirts, all spending the same weekend at the same hotel and convention center is all that matters.

We have just concluded four chapters using the Smythe family reunion as an analogy of the church. The purpose of those chapters was to remind ourselves that we need to take time to settle into a family that has been at it for quite a while. Many ministers have miserable experiences because they are too pigheaded to respect the mores of a family, to learn the family's habits, listen to the traditions, join in the festivities, and respect the cast of characters who have supported the clan across the years.

An equal but opposite way to have a disappointing ministry is to stay too long at the early get-acquainted stage of listening and acquiescence. At some point we are called to cast about for ways to help people see possibilities they have not seen before. Drawing largely on what we have perceived to be gifts and strengths already alive in the fellowship, we have been called to help the people in their growth, even at St. Smythes.

Arriving to look and listen, we evolve into a leader. We spend time prayerfully seeking the Lord's wisdom as we learn about this unique congregation, trying to discern what the quirks of God's vision for them might be. We try to sense the ways the Spirit is already at work defining an identity. We begin to foment a vision, not primarily by management/planning techniques, not by bringing in expert strategists, not by reading books or going to seminars. We help unleash the latent vision at the heart of the church by asking in every way possible one very simple question: "What kind of church does the Lord intend for us to be in this place?"

Our call is to get excited in the presence of our flock about questions like "What would happen if, when people united with this church and answered that Jesus Christ is their Lord and Savior, they really meant it?" "What would happen if we saw ourselves as a cadre of people the size of our membership roll, who had just arrived in town as missionaries?" "What would happen if we started to obey the first commandment about having no other gods before God?" "What would happen if serving the Lord through this church became a more urgent priority for us than our country club, our investment portfolio, our favorite sports team, our kid's soccer league, our social image in the community?" As we dream about how these questions might be answered, a thrill should sweep over us, driving our ministry. We begin to discern, as do some of the church's lay leadership, how we might answer the fundamental question: "What kind of church does the Lord intend for us to be in this place?" People begin to sense the vision that is within them.

Now, if all this were easily discerned and automatically carried out, I would not feel any urgency to sit here with a leaky pen and legal pad when I could be out walking the beach. (I write on vacation.)

There are, nonetheless, a few ideas that might help create an environment for vision. Let's look over a few hints as we evolve from looker/listener to leader/vision setter.

1. *Count our yeses.* We will not see too many churches where renewal is the result of moaning and groaning. Negativity does not lead to positive results. When we spend our time stewing over all the things that hold the church back, we usually miss the opportunities, the blessings, and the support that are right in front of our eyes. Our call is to spot and count our "yeses."

To put the thought in perspective, we need to remember that for most churches, practically every Sunday a majority of the members vote no to worship by not attending. We nonetheless hold worship for the yeses who elect to attend. Not only do we not follow the will of the negative majority, we center our church's life in the positive minority gathering to worship with us on any given Sunday.

The majority of first-time visitors to almost all of our churches will never join. In fact, a high percentage of them will never darken our door again. These people say no to us. Instead of being undone by this rejection, we offer new-member classes and welcome into our church family the yes people who have elected to unite with us.

The classic example of counting yeses is a financial campaign. If we listened to all the naysayers, we would never get the project off the ground. Our task is to seek out a few yes people who will promise their generous support. Then we can go to the congregation saying that our goal is $100,000, of which $50,000 has already been pledged. A few yeses will carry the church.

As we have been saying, our early months on the field should see us searching out what the Lord is already doing. Where is the spiritual renewal already under way? Where are the people with a heart for mission? Where is the interest in adult education? Where is "yes" already being whispered, spoken, or shouted in the church?

Rarely do we develop a vision to which people have not already in one way or another been saying yes for years. The yeses about the church and the yes people in the church are clues the Lord has laid out for us to help us find our vision.

2. *Be yes people ourselves.* We in ministry are plagued with the stereotype

of taking all the fun out of life. "The preacher" represents "Thou shalt not."
We are the ones who supposedly go around telling people what they are not
allowed to do. In fact, one reason why folks in churches are afraid to voice
new ideas is the fear that the highly judgmental reverend might be offended
and roar "NO" in an otherworldly voice.

So let's be yes people in the sense of permission givers. To our surprise we
might find that we become both a breath of fresh air and a complete revolutionary in an institution that might have been quite stingy about handing out
permission slips.

Soon after arriving in one of our former parishes Susan and I decided to
host a series of open houses in our home. We planned to invite the congregation in manageable numbers to attend, over whatever number of Sunday after-
noons it would take to cover the whole roll. In thinking about arrangements,
Susan recalled that the church owned several tablecloths that she knew would
be perfect for the open houses. Could she borrow them? I figured it should be
OK. I knew that there would certainly have been no problem in our former
congregation. I would simply have told the business manager that we were
going to borrow them, and that would have been that. We were in a new place,
and so I offered to scout out the protocol.

Big mistake. I inquired of my secretary about permission. She said it
sounded OK to her, but Susan had better check with the grounds committee
chair. Alas, I let the process unfold. I told Susan she might be wise to run it
past the grounds chair. He thought borrowing the tablecloths was a fine idea,
but said Susan should check with the woman's association chair. The
woman's association chair had no problem with the idea, but wondered if the
president of the trustees might have a problem. No problem there. Did the ruling body (session in a Presbyterian church) have a policy? The clerk said there
was no policy against it, but wondered if Christian education might already
have plans to use the tablecloths for one of their projects. The schedule was
clear. However, the Christian education chair told Susan she'd better check
with the woman who came in on a part-time basis to prepare meals for church
events. The woman did not know of any policy prohibiting the use of the
tablecloths and could think of no scheduling problems. But she did not like
the idea, so she said no and her no was final. Susan decided to use our own
tablecloths and toyed with becoming a Buddhist. This is why people say it is
easier to get forgiveness than permission in a church.

Without violating the rules of the congregation, our role should be that of
permission giver.

"Can we try this program?"

"Sure."

"We'd like to begin a new mission project. Can we?"

"Go for it."

Encourage it. Let it happen. Support it. Remove obstacles in the path, an important task. To say yes to a group seeking permission means (a) that we have to spell out for them places where permission needs to be given, and (b) we must be willing to stick our necks out to help get that permission. We do not want to say yes, and lead people into a disappointment.

Vision is hard to come by in many congregations because people don't dream dreams. They don't dream dreams because they don't feel they have permission. New ministries are not tried; new ideas are not brought up; new possibilities are not suggested for fear of doing the wrong thing and being a bad person.

In some ways our task is not so much to set the vision as to open the door that gives people permission to think new thoughts. Most vital churches have a yes person at the helm.

3. *Set up an organizational model that frees positive folks to lead.* Evidently negativity floats, because the naysayers sure seem to rise to the top. Without strong pastoral leadership the reins of a church may well wind up in the few hands of an overworked, though saintly core, who have so much church business on their plates they gag on even the thought of something new. Positive personalities when overworked become forces of negativity.

There is another problem. If we are not paying attention, power will drift into the hands of control freaks who earn the congregation's respect by doing everything, while conspicuously keeping every detail under their own control, which translates into their having power to say "no" to anything new.

This latter problem, especially, calls for a solution that is really quite obvious. We just go about acting according to denominational rules. We affirm our denomination's polity, which, in almost all mainline churches, vests power and authority in groups rather than individuals. "Yes, Virginia, the Holy Spirit acts through committees." There is a ruling board in every local church. This means they rule. They make their decisions on the basis of recommendations brought to them after being hammered out in committee meetings such as Christian education, worship, or mission.

We recognize that negativity and refusal to give permission stem from the same people having to serve on practically every committee, making them too tired and frazzled to toy with anything new. We also recognize that it stems from having a supereager person who has taken the reins of a committee and now circumvents the process to impose his (and in my experience it's usually a his) or her will. By making the denominational system work, we take a giant step toward solving these problems.

We broaden the base of committee involvement by asking persons who are not on the ruling board to serve on committees. This lowers the probability of individuals' being overworked. Suggesting that board members serve on only one committee helps them focus their attention. Filling committees with persons whose only church assignment is their particular committee increases the probability of excitement about new ideas. A carefully drawn up organizational model, with groups making recommendations to groups, leaves no room for control freaks who would govern by negative fiat. These persons are certainly welcome to be a part of a committee and submit both to *Robert's Rules of Order* and the voiced will of the committee. They are not free to control the process. Control freaks hate committees and will attack us for "all these committees." I respond, "What can I do? I'm Presbyterian." Strong committees control control freaks. These steps open the door wide for yeses to be uttered.

4. *Do well what we do.* If we have a vacancy on the ruling board, work with the nominating committee to seize the opportunity to make a good selection. If a staff vacancy exists, fill it with a highly talented and gifted person. If the church is going to have a program for a family-night supper, have an excellent program. If we are engaged in a building program and a lack of funds necessitates prioritizing, it is better to do only a fraction of the work in a first-class way than to do all of the work in a cheap, shoddy way.

Congregations often do not know how well they can do. They do not realize that they can be better and do better. The very process of doing what we do a little bit better than it used to be done goes a long way toward opening a church's eyes to see what more is possible. "You know, we can do better than we have been doing."

We live in a world that has been influenced by secularity but is hungry for spirituality. New people will visit our church as a step in their search for the Lord. If our worship is sloppy, our sermon thrown together at the last minute, our education second rate, our mission without focus, our building a mess, we may be responsible for thoughtlessly turning off a soul who was seeking God. We cannot be part of a renewal of faith if we ourselves don't care enough about it to do well the work of the church.

5. *Recruit new members.* Eventually we want the congregation itself to be a hospitable, inviting fellowship that draws new people into the family. This takes time and the overcoming of countless obstacles, as we will discuss in chapters 9 to 12.

Especially in our first year of looking and listening, we should set new members as a high priority. The very fact of bringing new people into the mix can do wonders to open the possibility for creative vision setting. So important is new blood that we should immediately look into how the church does the new-member process. Who are the people who do it? How is it done? Are there classes for new members? What is taught? Who are the teachers? We are likely to find no process at all and, if there is one, folks are usually more than happy to let us help, if not take over. New-member recruitment is one area we should be ready to take over if necessary in the early months. We make the follow-up calls. We do the inviting to the new-members' class. We teach it.

New people bring new ideas that can have a catalytic effect on the yeses already in place. A sizable new-members' class standing before the church family says, "Here we go." It says, "We are on the move." It will of course tweak a few naysayers who don't like change. More importantly, though, it will help unleash the yeses.

6. *Help the church become confident enough to take risks.* Did you know that we cannot walk without leaning forward, going off balance, or being momentarily about to fall? If our trailing leg does not come forward and catch us, we will fall flat on our face. If we are unable to take risks, especially the risk of falling flat, we cannot step forward. Following the analogy further, newborns are neither strong enough nor trusting enough to walk. It takes time to get to that moment when Mom holds receptive hands twelve inches from the tippy toddler and says, "Come to Mommy." The first halting step is tried, usually resulting in an unceremonious kerplunk on the diapered end of the matter. Gradually, the baby learns that the other foot can come forward and help regain balance. Gradually, the baby walks.

Churches are the same way. At first we take a halting little step of a chance. Little failures are not big catastrophes. Why not get in the habit of printing a few more bulletins in the hope that more people will attend worship, even if we risk having to throw extras away? Why not plan for success? Why not run the not-so-outlandish risk of brewing extra coffee for those new people we expect to show up? In fact, are not the new members themselves something of a pleasant risk that the family must face, to which it must adjust, and from which it might learn?

As a calculated risk in a former church, I announced that I would be teaching a very elementary Bible class. In preparation for it, I asked that 125 notebooks be ordered. Voices from the finance department were heard to protest, "We won't have that many people in class, and we'll be stuck paying for unused books." Fortunately by then the church had witnessed the positive results of the less-than-high-wire act of printing more bulletins and brewing more coffee. Folks figured we should be able to risk this one, though the more cautious among us still wanted us to order only between twenty-five and forty books. When four hundred people signed up and we had to scurry at the last minute to get 275 more notebooks, the notion of risk found itself a supporting illustration.

If we cannot grow together to the point where we tilt forward in risk, the Lord can never teach us to walk.

What we are saying is that we make a transition from listening to leading, not by drafting a vision statement or a long-range planning report, but by adjusting attitudes and procedures. A positive permission-giving style in a committee-driven polity frees a church to seek the best, to take necessary risks, and to go for it.

Churches, like families, get rather set in their ways. Even parishes that bemoan how bad it has been and how anxious they are to soar to new heights are, in spite of their claims, quite comfortable in their complaining and in their "how bad it has been" normalcy. They really aren't so sure what soaring is anyway. Besides, the "how bad it has been" church is cheap and less likely to change their lives. So church people don't readily appreciate what they could possibly become. They assume this is as good as it gets. Our task is to free up the visionaries and then help them focus their vision.

Chapter 6

Accountability

Some years ago I read about a football team that was quite successful. The writer was evidently a friend of the coach, a friendship that resulted in an invitation to come to practices, follow the team through its weekly routine, and attend games with 50-yard-line seats.

In trying to figure out why this team won, the author was struck by the team's poise. They played well under pressure. With the game on the line, a jammed stadium rocking with crowd noise, millions of people watching on TV, this team was at its best every time.

How was this possible? Why weren't they rattled by the crowd? How did they keep their composure and play so successfully in the moments of greatest stress?

The author wrote that he discovered the secret when he followed the routine of this squad in the days following the game. Evidently, the team would sit down with the coaching staff and review films of the game play by play, player by player. If someone missed a block, it was pointed out. If someone not only made his block but went the extra mile by blocking an additional player, praise was lavished. The writer noted how the players hung on their coach's every word.

There was the secret. When they had to march down the field to score a touchdown with victory or defeat hanging in the balance, the team was not awed by the gargantuan players on the other side of the line. They were not rattled by the crowd noise. They were not even thinking about the millions of people staring at them on millions of TV screens. They knew that in only a matter of hours they would be in the film room being evaluated by their coach. He had trained them and conditioned them to know what to do and how to do it. Now they had to execute the game plan or be severely judged. They could keep their heads and play to the peak of their ability because they knew for whom they played the game. They knew to whom they were accountable. They played the game for the coach, and they played it well.

From time to time I pose a question to our ruling board. "To whom or to what are we accountable?" In football parlance, we are asking, "For whom are we playing the game?"

Interestingly enough, the answer may vary depending largely on the setting in which the question is posed. If we are seated casually in a circle drinking coffee at a Saturday morning training event with no difficult issue to be debated, the session members may seek an answer that they think will be "right." Having witnessed more than their share of children's sermons, they know that the answer to every pastor's question posed to the kiddos is either "Jesus," "God," or "love." They ponder what to say that will please us pastors. Since we asked the question, they will figure one of the children's-sermon answers is the "right" answer, which will make us happy. Amid this relaxed, low-threat-level banter, they are content to mouth something about Jesus, God, or love, not paying too much attention to their own words.

If, however, we raise the question "To whom are we accountable?" at a board meeting when people are hunched over their papers, elbows on the table, hassling over a most urgent, controversial issue, they are less interested in what the pastor thinks is the right answer. Religious jargon takes a back seat. This is serious. In this setting they bark out what they really believe. "We are accountable to the people who elected us to this session and to the people who pay the bills around here."

Controversial discussion rarely sneaks up on us. We usually know, coming into the room, we have a hot potato on the agenda. There has usually been a build-up to the meeting. The hot issue has been the subject of phone calls, conversation at social events in the community, and debates in the hallways of the church. Session members have received an earful before coming to the meeting. They feel as if they have been sent to do the bidding of the particular people who have been haranguing them for days, if not weeks. They know that if the session votes a certain way, their friends will explode at them in anger. As a consequence, some board members will not be readily open to debate. They will feel themselves to be under oppressive pressure. It is vital to their social well-being to be able to tell their friends, "At least *I* voted *our* way."

Don't get me wrong. The will of the congregation cannot be taken lightly. After all, we are a people who believe in collective wisdom. When we seek the truth about the mysteries of life we do not climb to the mountaintop to find some bearded guru in a white robe. We gather God's people in one room to pray, discuss, get into Scripture, and then engage in prayerful deliberation.

After this, we take a vote. So, if the will of the congregation is clearly on one side of an issue, it needs to be taken seriously. These are, after all, God's people who have confessed their faith in Jesus Christ as their Lord and Savior.

What the ruling board needs to grasp is that, while we take the input of the congregation with great seriousness, perhaps even wondering if the Lord might be speaking to us through the will of the congregation, we are to see ourselves quite differently from politicians who have been elected to represent their constituents.

When the pressure is on, we have an opportunity to explain that the difference between board members elected by the congregation and representatives elected by their constituents is that board members are ordained. Elected officials are not. Ordination involves the laying on of hands, the setting apart for a sacred office. When we are set apart, we are given a whole new accountability. We are to take the will of the congregation seriously, but we are accountable to the Lord. In our meetings we begin with prayer and devotions. No one wonders if such praying is a violation of church-state relations. Of course we pray. We want to be explicitly in touch with the One to whom we are accountable. We deliberate on agenda matters to seek God's will. We seek to discern what Scripture teaches. We may call for more prayer. All that we do is to the end of seeking the will of God and having the courage to follow it.

I have often felt that the most important role I play in session meetings is to be ready at the right times to remind the board members whose we are. Left to themselves, many folks will take seriously the will of God but understand themselves accountable to the congregation. Our task is repeatedly to remind them that we take seriously the will of the congregation but are accountable to God.

What a blessing it is to have lay leaders who speak with a voice of spiritual integrity rather than political expediency when a tough issue is being discussed! These people join us in keeping accountabilities straight. I recall a time when the church I served was on the list of congregations targeted for Sunday morning demonstrations by dissident steelworkers. The demonstrators had already disrupted services at other churches, and our announced turn for disruption was fast approaching. It was a tense moment for us. The mood of our session was to call in the troops to protect the church from the invading hordes. Some people were suggesting we bring in the National Guard. For a time it appeared our session would ask to have armed guards at the door. One voice in the room turned the tide. One man spoke about how the Lord was calling us to minister to the poor. He reminded us all that the demonstrators were offering their protest as a cry of anguish uttered out of poverty, unemployment, and despair. That night all of us knew that our colleague backed up his words with action, because we knew he had already gone out of his way to hire persons who had been put out of work when the local mills had been shut down. He spoke out of a life accountable to Jesus. His words had a "Thus says the Lord" ring to them. At one of the most critical moments in my ministry he was a voice reminding us that our ultimate allegiance is to the One who came not to be served but to serve. He turned us toward an open, welcoming, hospitable witness that permitted tremendous strides in mission we could not possibly have foreseen in those days of heated discussions. For his efforts, I am eternally grateful.

The result within our congregation was eye-opening. We found that only after we had freed ourselves from being accountable to the congregation's perceived will could we see what their actual will really was. Our surface impression had been that the congregation wanted us to be tough. While no doubt some members of the church did indeed wish that, at heart, the church members were praying that we would do the right thing. What they really wanted was for us to have a witness that reflected their faith in Jesus Christ. For all the pontificating and efforts to influence the process toward toughness, the overwhelming majority of parishioners turned out to be looking to the church's leadership to be Christlike.

Let's be clear about this. Following the will of God is not defined one way or the other by the perceived will of the congregation. It is, however, helpful to note that when we cut through all the shouting and posturing, we find that Christ's church wants to be Christ's church. It is the will of the congregation that their leaders make decisions in concert with the will of God and not the perceived will of the congregation. They know in their hearts that the only way to be fully Christ's church is not to make decisions based on how the members seem to feel. We become Christ's church by seeking and following the will of Christ.

We can learn a valuable lesson for our local congregations by drawing on denominational experience. Some years ago I was a delegate to our denomination's annual meeting (General Assembly). As testimony to what a mover and shaker I am, I was a member of a subcommittee of a subcommittee in an area I would not have chosen for myself. In fact I don't even recall exactly what we did. I do recall the tone with which we did it. In our first meeting, strong voices were heard to say that we dared not make certain decisions or utter certain pronouncements lest "the folks back home" be offended. "They sent us here. Let's not turn them off." We began with a solid desire to do the bidding of the parishioners in congregations across the denomination.

By our third meeting, the worm had turned. Perhaps some of our number had had a chance to sleep on it. Perhaps they had discussed the matter outside our subcommittee of the subcommittee. At any rate, voices were now heard saying that we needed to have courage. We were elected to make decisions for ourselves according to our consciences. We were not beholden to what the folks back home wanted. We must not let them close our minds or dictate what we should decide. We must be free to make whatever decisions we felt we should make, and if that offended people, so be it.

Now the subcommittee of the subcommittee was getting fired up. Now there was fire in the eyes of many around our small circle. When a matter came up for discussion, some among us began measuring the wisdom of an idea by how offensive it would seem to "the folks back home." The more offensive it was, the more proper. For the notion that we should reflect the will of our congregations back home, the delegates had substituted an equal but opposite concept that we should never do the will of those congregations.

Happily, we had enough time to work through our Hegelian thesis/antithesis to another plane of thought, which was not so much a synthesis as it was a realization that the will of the congregation (thesis) and the anti–will of the congregation (antithesis) were both matters to be considered, but neither reflected our accountability. We were accountable to God. Sometimes God leads us in a path that pleases the constituency. Sometimes God leads us down a path that offends. Other times the Lord leads in a direction that draws no reaction at all. We are to follow the Lord's lead regardless of whether "the folks back home" like it or not.

This, my friends, is what makes us Christians dangerous. This is why, when we let an open process elect people to the denomination's ruling bodies and people come with a willingness to pray and deliberate, the Lord can have at us in ways that may turn out to be quite startling. What makes Christians dangerous is that the Lord can be Lord, and the Lord is uncontrollable.

I worry when I see people trying to stack the deck of delegates to our annual meeting so that one side or the other will have the balance of power in a culture war debate. To paraphrase Jesus, we cannot be accountable to two masters. We cannot be accountable to God and to our colleagues who sent us to do their bidding in a culture war vote. We cannot be accountable to God if we are not willing to come into the Lord's courts with a willingness to let God change our minds. Some of us had hoped that calling our denomination to a sabbatical from one culture war debate in the late 1990s would give us time to become accountable to the Lord instead of ecclesiastical action groups.

When we let ourselves be accountable to God, we are quite dangerous and quite exciting. A great disservice has been done to the mainline denominational church in recent years by our grouping ourselves into camps. We go into the deliberative process representing our people, arguing for our cause, referring to our group's research, drawing on the wisdom of our group's best minds. We go not to deliberate, but to politic, hoping to defeat those who have a view different from our own. We go into denominational deliberation with a mind-set akin to going into battle. In the process we lose our capacity to bring people to their knees in awe. We don't cause folks to shudder anymore in the presence of an awesome truth revealed through us. We've lost our ability to say, "Thus says the Lord."

The sanctuary was jammed where a regional meeting (presbytery) was being held. This was the year our denomination made headlines when it was revealed that a committee had granted $10,000 to the defense of Angela Davis, an avowed Communist accused of murder. Parishioners were up in arms. The press was showing its uncanny ability both to misunderstand the situation and simultaneously to inflame a community.

In that environment we met to make a statement. The discussion was running true to form, only with far more passion than usual. We heard from the side that thought we should frame a statement to comfort the folks back home and keep their pocketbooks open. Others, of course, felt it our call to offend.

The debate was spiraling nowhere when an African American pastor, veteran of many a heated moment, asked to speak. He strode to the center pulpit, Scriptures in hand. Dramatically, he opened his Bible and set it on the pulpit. Looking us in the eye, he said, "Now let's see what our Lord Jesus has to say about this." With that, a burden was lifted. The reaction of the folks back home ceased to control us. The press could go on missing the point for all we cared. We were going to listen to Jesus, be guided by our Lord, and follow the Lord's leading.

When we decided that day to let God be God, we knew most anything could happen. We did not yet know exactly what we were going to do. All we knew was that it was going to be compassionate, inclusive, just, and fearlessly aligned with the downtrodden. For a marvelous moment, we became accountable to God. We became uncontrollably dangerous. For a brief moment, the courts of the church were alive and exhilarating.

Chapter 7

Reforming

*F*rom seminary days to the moment I sit scratching out these thoughts on a legal pad, my ministry has been conducted in the light of a motto: "Always reformed, always reforming." I know this is a big phrase for Presbyterians, such as your author. Perhaps this explains my fondness for ecclesiastical schizophrenia. In the simplest of terms, I read the adage to be saying that we believe an eternal, unchangeable truth called "the Reformed tradition." At the same time, we are always to be tinkering with it. No wonder we get headaches. We dare to proclaim a theology that never changes, while our mission is to keep forever changing our version of it. Such a predicament is not just Presbyterian. It crosses all denominational lines.

My seminary professors might not recognize the theology they tried to run past my inattentive mind. I have found what for me is a very helpful way of interpreting the "always reformed, always reforming" idea.

Let's begin with the notion of idolatry. The first two commandments are on that subject. While the Second Commandment is quite explicitly about idolatry, with its injunction not to make or bow down to graven images, it is commandment number one that sets the tone. "You shall have no other gods before me" (Ex. 20:3). Having any other god is idolatry. Taking anything in the creation with the seriousness that should be reserved for the Creator alone is to practice idolatry as much as if we carved an image of a duck and bowed to it every morning.

When we say that we are "always reformed," we are saying that we trust in the sovereignty of God and the centrality of Jesus Christ. We put first things first. We have no other gods before the Lord God. We love the Lord with all our heart, with all our soul, and with all our mind. Our theology, our preaching, and our ministry are based on the basic truth that God is God, indeed God alone is God.

Because we are sinful critters who see through a glass dimly, we inevitably get carried away with lesser gods. Often for lofty motives, we get all excited about good things that are themselves very much a part of the Christian life. Sometimes we take what is very good and treat it as though it were God. When that happens, the second half of our adage clicks in. Then it is that we need to be "always reforming," reforming our lives so that the good thing, which is not God, is put back in its place and only God is worshiped as God. In other words, to be always reformed we must constantly be reforming our sinful lives, removing our idolatries so that God will again be God.

To make sense of this admittedly confusing distinction, let's play it out. Suppose that on vacation we read a stimulating book on urban ministry. We get excited. We become convinced that the hand of God is guiding our suburban congregation toward the inner city. Near the close of vacation we happen to worship at a church that has all kinds of posters and bulletin announcements interpreting their ministry in a city several miles away. We sense that the Lord is trying to tell us something. We return home fired up to lead our congregation into urban work.

Our sermons through September touch on our need to get beyond the walls of our church and the borders of our town. By World Communion Sunday we have set the stage for our blockbuster "Let's Do Urban Ministry" sermon. Despite our fears that we would be called a bleeding heart or a liberal commie pinko, the message is well received. People are itching to get on with it. There is a buzz in the church about working with the city.

A phone call to a colleague in a downtown church leads to a lunch. She loves the idea of our churches' entering a partnership. We exchange pulpits. Our choirs do a joint concert. Our youth groups fellowship together. A task force is established to set up a tutoring program for urban children and to start a food pantry to be located in the basement of the downtown church building.

Our people are loving it. What's not to love? It is a worthy ministry. Every Thursday night a team of tutors goes downtown. The first Sunday of every month an entire corner of the fellowship hall is filled with bags of groceries for the food pantry. The Tuesday morning men's prayer breakfast group delivers them. The adult education committee has developed a series of classes on urban issues. The mission committee has designated funds for our partner church so that they can hire a seminary assistant. Permission is granted to take an occasional special offering to meet emergencies in the urban parish. People are giving voluntary testimonies in the halls of the church, telling how this urban outreach has changed their lives. They share how their attitudes have done a 180-degree turn since they've seen "how many advantages we have that our brothers and sisters in the city do not." Denominational leaders are lauding our two churches for providing a model of cooperation. We are on top of the world.

Then some difficulties arise. The initial roster of tutors has had some normal attrition and now there is difficulty recruiting replacements. People are just too busy to volunteer for another night out. Then the budget crunch hits. Pledges are in and some cuts are needed. Mission had asked for an increase in funding for urban support. The property committee has been planning for five years to recarpet the second floor of the Christian education building. The choir wants new robes for the children. Last year the new-members committee had to cut its funding for a church brochure and they are "sick and tired of being treated like second-class citizens around here." There are even some voices saying that the urban ministry has "taken over the church." Mind you, all of this is fairly normal for a church at budget-cutting time.

We would not think much of it, except for some phrases dropped in the mission committee meeting when the budget is discussed. "The property committee is so selfish." "People who are too busy to volunteer one night a week tutoring city kids have their priorities all wrong." "How can you call yourself a Christian and not see that this is the Lord's work?" "We've got a lot of people in this church who don't know what discipleship is." "I'm going to withdraw my pledge from this church and give it all to urban ministry." "This ministry is the most important thing in my life."

Our role is important here. Of course we continue to give our full support to the urban dialogue. It is our baby, and we can legitimately be expected to be on the side of folks ministering to the city. At the same time, we need to be guardians at the edge of idolatry. The reformed call to mission sometimes needs to be balanced by the reforming reminder that this particular mission, while wonderful, is not God. In other words ministry is a terribly difficult balancing act of getting people enthused about a particular work, but not so narrowly enthused that the work becomes an idol.

For a mission committee to engage in its own brand of church hyperbole is not unnatural. Some strong language is to be expected. Concern arises when people voice the thought that this project is the sign of being a Christian, as if one were saved by signing up to work with us. We are on dangerous turf when people begin to use their devotion to a particular project as the issue that separates God's people from the heathen. We have then entered unhealthy territory, and the enthusiasm needs a dose of theological reality. Remember, folks: Our work is in service to God. It is not itself God.

We are quite good at spotting the sliver in our neighbor's eye on matters like this. We feel that the Lord is offering a prophetic word through us when we challenge the idolatrous loyalty some of our parishioners have for the American flag. We point out with gusto the idolatrous way people pledge their allegiance to the stock market, or the local restrictive zoning. We lift up for scrutiny the religious passion with which families give themselves to their children's athletic teams. Ours is a message that points out the idolatries of our community. We rather enjoy challenging those folks to be about the business of reforming, so that God, and only God, will be God. Where we are not so comfortable or competent is in recognizing the mote in our own eye, idolatries that have put a stranglehold on our own minds and ministries.

Perhaps we are blinded by the fact that, as with the urban project, we are very much engaged in what is so clearly God's will. We can be so self-righteously revved up to charge off doing what we are convinced is God's will that we fail to note when the power of evil uses our momentum to push us across an invisible line. We have allowed doing God's will on this project to become for us more important than God. Without noticing, we let our cause become the judge and/or the savior of us all. As we listen to our own rhetoric, we may hear words questioning the faith of those who oppose us. We hear voices in our camp say, "Fred is unbiblical. He just doesn't have Jesus in his heart." Reminded that Fred has publicly accepted Jesus Christ as his Lord and Savior, our cohort says, "If Jesus were really his Lord and Savior, Fred would be on our side in urban ministry." Or perhaps we hear, "Maggie is my idea of a Christian." Informed that Maggie never attends church, and has made no bones about professing her agnosticism, our crony says, "Maggie is really a citizen of God's kingdom because she works with our group in the city."

The problem here is not in declaring that God's disciples are those who walk the walk even more than those who merely talk the talk. The problem is that we have let our project become a god of judgment and salvation. If you are with us, you are saved. If you are against us, you are doomed. If we do nothing more in our ministries than call ourselves and our sisters and brothers to reform our thinking about our projects and positions, to remind ourselves that our urban ministry is not God, that only God is God, then we will have done wonders to advance the peace, unity, and purity of the church, while affirming anew what it is to be reformed.

Let's run our thinking through three further examples.

1. *Lens.* Over the years of my ministry, the church has gone through many theological incarnations. We have had the cost of discipleship and religion-less Christianity, secular cities and new theologies, the theologies of hope, stewardship of the environment, liberation theology, black theology, feminist theology. All of these have grown out of a genuine faith, biblical research, and a felt need in the midst of human life. My consciousness has been raised and my faith deepened by them all.

I recall how I would get excited about the theological idea that was the buzz word at church gatherings. I would begin to see all of Scripture, all of life, all of God's nature through what we call the "lens" of hope or stewardship. Inevitably, my colleagues and I found that sermons and church school classes took their cues from "the theology." Unwittingly, in our excitement about "the theology" we narrowed our concept of God. We developed an idolatrous dependence on our theological catchword.

In God's limitless mercy, we have found that, when we get too carried away with "the theology," the church rises up to reform itself. We collectively realize that, while hope and stewardship are very crucial to a vital faith, they do not sum up the faith. God is bigger than our theological perspective, however helpful it has been to us.

C. S. Lewis once observed that God is love. Scripture tells us that. However, love is not God. Only God is God. To make love God is to make an idol of love.

Inevitably, God comes to us through a lens, but the lens is not God.

That we should read the Bible through our own particular lens is not wrong. Each of us has a lens that enables us to get a handle on the whole of God's Word. Some of us look at the Bible as a manual spelling out a plan of salvation. Others of us see God's revelation as an articulation of grace. Still others among us see ministry to the poor and marginalized as the lens through which to read the whole. In my own spiritual experience, I have found that "justice love," for all the turmoil to which it has led, is about as good as any lens. In fact I find it the best and most helpful for me.

The challenge is to keep in mind the vastness of God and the limitation of a lens. A lens through which we view a sunset is not the sunset, nor can it capture the full grandeur of the sunset. I do not abuse Paul's intent when I say, "For now we see in a lens dimly, but then we will see face to face" (1 Cor. 13:12). For all the inevitability of viewing Scripture through our own lens, for all the cohesive clarity that comes from knowing what our lens is, we too often find ourselves with an idolatrous reliance on our lens, which is not God. We can quite easily worship what is by definition a limitation of truth, a selector, a shading of truth. We can treat our lens as if it were God.

2. *Ministerial success.* We would rather not think about it. But we must ask whether our commitment to this institution called local congregation, or our vision for that church, or our homegrown projects have taken the place of God in our lives? Are we mouthing words about the sovereignty of God and the centrality of Jesus while we are really looking to the building program or the next new-members' class to be our savior? Are we preaching the grace of God while excluding from our list of the faithful anyone who is not with us on some project or other? Are we urging people to accept the free gift of salvation offered in Christ, while we really want persons to show their Christianity by upping

their pledge or helping us increase our attendance statistics? Don't most of us need to be about the task of reforming our idolatrous commitment to a successful church?

3. *Self.* Our final example draws blood. Is it possible that the ministry has itself become a means to serve the chief end of our lives—namely, ourselves? Is it because the line between psychotherapy and ministry has been so blurred that we look to the ministry to be the context in which we can find ourselves, be ourselves, be fulfilled, be actualized, and have a comfortable working environment? Can you imagine the apostle Paul demanding that he have a comfortable working environment or he'll call the denomination's committee on ministry? I could imagine his therapist, if he had one, counseling him to find a comfortable working environment. I cannot imagine the One who has called us to ministry ever suggesting such a thing.

The fact that too many among us measure the integrity of our call in terms of whether we are happy on this particular field of service, the fact that too many among us spend too much time focusing on how we are treated by our congregation, the fact that too many among us talk about our rights instead of our responsibilities are signs that idolatry of self is alive and well among the clergy.

The idolatry of self is extremely destructive in staff relations. A new person on staff might do well to read our first four chapters and apply the patient looking and listening techniques to the process of fitting in with the team that is already in place. Instead, we find otherwise capable persons playing victim, crying about rights, rounding up congregational support for "me." Rarely do I run into persons serving in a staff-led church where I do not hear about major problems that threaten to blow the congregation apart. We dare not be simplistic about the highly complex dynamics of staff turmoil. My observation is that far too much of it takes its root in one or more (and it is usually more) persons on staff taking themselves far too seriously. Nowhere do we need to be more intentional in our work of reforming than we do with our own idolatrous worship of our own sinful egos.

In other words, can we call ourselves reformed if we are not first and foremost rigorous in the work of reforming our own lives and our own ministries?

Chapter 8

Priorities

Some years ago, in a presbytery I won't name, I served on a committee whose task it was to coordinate the entire justice, social action, and race relations ministries of the region. Our committee was one of those monsters created by restructuring. The racism task force, the women's issues task force, the employment, hunger, justice, and social outreach task forces had all been lumped together in one group. Clearly this was a top-priority responsibility demanding our very best efforts.

I must admit I was uncharacteristically eager to attend the meeting, for which I was unavoidably fifteen minutes late. When I entered the room, I found the group smaller than I had anticipated. About seven or eight folk were already engrossed in a discussion. Sorry to be tardy, I was anxious to pick up on the nature of the subject and see if I might be able to add to the conversation. Now I want you to understand I'm not making this up. It really happened. Apparently one of our members had lobbied presbytery to have a half-hour presentation at their next meeting. I thought this might be a bit premature, since we had no known ideas to bring forth. I listened to see what we might be able to come up with for our time on the agenda. (Don't laugh.) A couple of our committee members had asked three women to do a chancel dance for our half hour. Evidently our task force, having no better idea and never questioning the need for us to have a half hour of agenda time at so early a stage of our work, had already bought into the concept by the time I arrived. The entire justice and social action work of our task force would be captured by these three women doing whatever they planned to do in their leotards on the chancel floor. The better part of the remainder of our meeting was taken up by a discussion of where we would get the seventy-five dollars required to pay these women to do whatever it was they would do.

An urgently needed task force of a major presbytery surrounding a major and in many ways hurting city was using our meeting time trying to find seventy-five bucks to pay three dancers!

It is not for me to question the importance of the chancel dancers. Frankly, chancel dance is not important to me, though I'll admit it does seem important to some people. Evidently, there are people who have found such dancing to be spiritually uplifting. Fine. I just wasn't convinced that night nor am I convinced now that spending the time of so crucial a task force hassling over seventy-five dollars for dancers was the best use of our time.

Our subject is priorities. With all the diverse and often seemingly random demands for our time and energy, how do we get enough possession of ourselves to set priorities? Just as important, if not more so, how do we carry out our ministry in a way consistent with our priorities? How on earth can we conduct our ministries based on our priorities without offending our congregation, who are constantly coming at us with priorities of their own? And, if we have arrived at a church where our model of the church is a family reunion, are there not limits on the appropriateness of setting our own priorities anyway? Don't we know of ruined ministries where a friend of ours, like a bull in a china shop, barged in to impose priorities on a fellowship that already had its own priorities and did not cotton to new ones?

Several principles emerge.

1. We are well advised not to draw a distinction publicly between the important and the unimportant. Most of what goes on in the church family has its own importance to somebody. To some members of that presbytery committee, and to several members of the presbytery, interpretive chancel dance is very important. For me to attempt to make a case that it is not important would be an exercise in the ludicrous. Further, the budgeting process is important. While I thought squabbling over seventy-five dollars in a presbytery that should be thinking in the millions was a trivial matter, I could not say the discussion was unimportant. We are well served to have an extremely broad concept of what is important.

2. The more helpful distinction is not between important and unimportant; it is between important and priority. In the book of Acts we read that the early church faced a problem in the deployment of its leadership. Pastoral care lacked coordination. This very important part of the church's ministry was leaving many people feeling neglected. The apostles realized how important pastoral ministry was. Their priority was teaching. In order to give themselves to their priority, they appointed other people, including Stephen, the first Christian martyr, to take charge of the very important matter of pastoral work (Acts 6:1–6).

Our challenge in this calling of ours is to function as one person in a work where there is enough important business to occupy ten of our clones on a full-time basis. We can try to explain this to people in a way that is gracious and inclusive. "While this project of yours is very important to the church, my priority has to be over here, where I am called to spend the bulk of my time, energy, and imagination." I will not guarantee that the words will be warmly received. Together we can work to follow the model from Acts. We can devise procedures for helping people recruit workers to accomplish the important. In so doing, we free ourselves to do our priority.

3. Let's be careful with this next point. We bring to our church our own priorities, which have been chosen independent of this particular congregation and which are not wholly subject to the congregation's opinion. The apostles decided without consulting the congregation to let Stephen and the deacons do the pastoral work. Scripture does not give details of what the church thought of the idea. No doubt some folks wanted to get their food basket from Peter instead of Stephen. If they did, it did not seem to matter, because the apostles had a basic and legitimate priority to which they had committed themselves. Wedded to their priority, they did not have time for the important.

When we graduated from seminary, a friend of mine was called to be pastor of a three-hundred-member congregation. On his arrival, he asked the ruling board, "Now that I'm here, what do you want me to do?" One person spoke for the group. "Son, if you don't know what your job is, you'd better pack up and get out of town." A born leader, my friend took that as his wake-up call. He realized people expect us to have an idea what we are doing. They expect us to know what our priorities are and to give ourselves to acting on them.

Mind you, this is no invitation to self-serving arrogance on our part. Nor can we assume that, just because our church expects us to know our priorities, they will automatically approve wholeheartedly. (Remember, I said, "Let's be careful on this point.") We can anticipate that if we dedicate ourselves to preaching and teaching, folks may wish we were more pastoral. They may accuse us of being administratively inept. If we are primarily dedicated to pastoral care, there might be an uprising by those who think we should spend more time on our sermons, and again we may appear administratively inept. If we see administration as our thing, they may see us as aloof and Machiavellian. There will always be some folks who wish our priorities were elsewhere. They may even be able to remind us of a predecessor or staff member who was "a real minister," that is to say, "had the right priorities" in our critic's opinion.

4. Our call is to help a congregation come to a very general understanding of its collective priorities and show how our priorities mesh with theirs. The

fact of the matter is that the presbytery committee I mentioned earlier was giving too much of its time, energy, and imagination to a nonpriority issue. Though I could tell by the intensity of the discussion that the subject was very important to some people, I would argue it was a waste of priority agenda time. That the committee thus misspent its time is the fault of the presbytery for not giving us clearer direction, of the chair for letting it happen, and, yes, it is my fault for being unwilling to risk their ire by helping them redirect their focus. Somebody needed to take hold of that group and help it find its priorities.

A reason we should spend our first year in a church looking and listening is so that we can ferret out from among the umpteen important aspects of a congregation's life what are the sacred priorities that give meaning to that congregation. We need to remember that the church already has priorities that can be readily discerned if we'll just look and listen. After one such year of observation, I formed the conclusion that the particular fellowship I then served saw its reason for being on planet Earth as threefold: They provided a location for a local scout troop to hold all their activities. They were proud to rally a tremendous number of parishioners, mostly women, to hold an annual sale of everything from baked goods to used clothing. The money went to mission, and they raised plenty of it. Thirdly, they conducted and housed an excellent summer event for children. That was it.

Mess with the scouts at your own risk. Reschedule them, ask them to use another room, or move their stuff, and we'd be branded a strange person who didn't care about values. Even think about curbing any aspect of the fall sale and they'd show us the door. We could not even start Sunday school until well into October, lest Sunday school interfere with the sale. It was assumed from the order of creation that the kids' program in the summer ruled. Nothing could compete with it, distract from it, or question it.

Mind you, all these activities were important. People worked very diligently over long hours to accomplish them. Great good was done in the lives of many people because of them. My ministry was greatly aided by taking the time to realize these were the priority items for that congregation. I could then affirm these programs, lend my support to them, and in time even get the people to see where some changes needed to be made. For example, the summer program involved a lot of outdoor activity and athletic competition. My first year there, I learned in the post-camp evaluation that because of the program's athletic requirements the mother of a little boy with a physical handicap was told her son would not be admitted to our program. He had to stay home. Since he could not compete, he did not belong.

My response was, shall we say, less than favorable. We spent some time with our church's camp leadership team discussing the fact that Jesus did not invite the able-bodied children to come to him. He invited the children. Period. Couldn't the church of Jesus Christ find a way to make some adjustments so that all the children could come to the Lord in this, our church's best-known children's program? To their credit, leadership was more than willing to accommodate. This was no easy task. Since we were all of one mind in wanting this program to be a witness to Jesus, the staff put in the time to change the requirements and adjust the style to be more inclusive. The program is still going strong. And get this: Ten years into my ministry there were very few dry eyes in the room when a precious little girl, a quadriplegic, won the camper of the year award.

As we are affirming and sharing in the church's existing priorities, we are gradually introducing priorities of our own. We need to be clear. We cannot think that any priority of ours is OK for us to push on the unsuspecting saints. Unless we are called to an unusual church, we had better take stock of ourselves and accept only the most basic of priorities for our ministries.

When I was younger and my body was limber enough to move about with a modicum of ease, I loved to play softball. If the Lord had ordained that the purpose of a church is to get up teams for a softball league, this boy would have been one happy camper. In fact, in the first two churches I served as pastor we got a team into the church league. (For the reader who recalls my play on these teams, understand that I am saying I loved playing. I am not saying I was all that good.) In my second church we even had uniforms. Man, that was cool! I pitched, and we even won a few games with me on the mound. Our team got into the play-offs. And we didn't even have any ringers!

Obviously the softball league was very important to me. Everyone knew I loved it. The players and their families loved it. It was important to all of us. We also knew that it was not a priority of ministry. Unless we start a new church with an explicit mandate to initiate a softball ministry, softball is not to be a priority.

If our passion is drama, or retreats, or twelve-step programs, or small groups, or clown ministry, or rock music, we are best served coming clean with the search committee that is calling us. We should meet with the ruling board and the proper denominational committee to let them all know of our passion, especially if it is so strong a passion that it will inevitably be a priority. If the congregation shows little receptivity, we should not accept the call. Priorities are that important. If we cannot work with the church family at the priority level, our ministry will suffer.

As I enter the late afternoon of my ministry, I realize that everywhere I have served my priorities have been the same. In the early years, I did not think about it. I just did it. The priorities were subconscious, implicit. Now they are conscious and explicit. They have not changed. Fortunate for my ministry, they have been very, very basic, resonating with the heartbeat of every congregation I have served, in fact every congregation I have ever encountered.

My priorities for whatever Smythe family reunion of a congregation I am called to pastor are that the church serve the Lord through worship, education, and mission in a context of hospitality.

My experience has been that church members are becoming more comfortable with God-talk. When I was ordained in the 1960s many people were hesitant about mentioning "God," or "Lord," or "Jesus." We were pressured to be relevant and modern. We dared not look like religious fanatics or be so heavenly-minded that we were no earthly good. We were secular and street-savvy. "Serving the Lord" was at best an implicit goal for many of my generation. We could say "serving," but we could not say "Lord."

Over the intervening years a spiritual hunger has ached within the church. While in the '60s we would have been hooted out of the room if we offered words like "The Lord has done something in my life," now we can come right out and talk about God. We are more God-conscious. Now, when I talk God-talk, people want to hear it. When we think about serving the Lord, a resounding yes is felt in the room. "Show us how." I feel an increasingly close bond with members of the church family when I think out loud about serving the Lord. In fact, I never saw a church information form in the format we Presbyterians used to use where any local church did not check "spiritual development of members" as a top priority. I don't need to fuss and fume and use manipulative tricks to cajole a church into desiring to "serve the Lord." All I need to do is open the door.

The door opens primarily through worship. Worship is a priority. Because worship is a priority, I make preaching a priority. Every week my ministry is structured around one thing: preparing the sermon to be delivered the following Sunday. Each day interruptions take me away from working on the sermon, and so I am constantly looking ahead to guarantee that I will have the time needed for what will happen through the pulpit Sunday morning.

In the particular church I discussed a few paragraphs back, where scouts, a fall sale, and a summer program were their top priorities, I did not mention worship as a priority. This is not because they did not want to emphasize worship. It was because they did not believe it possible for worship to be a cornerstone of their life together. Worship attendance stood at 15 percent of the membership.

This is no reason to write off worship as a priority. It is reason to affirm it as an unrealized and unspoken priority. Church people in all churches want to worship. They want to hear God's Word proclaimed. They want to be led in prayer. They want to be inspired by the music of the church. Get this: They want to come to church. They may not want to come sit through the sloppy, second-rate palaver some of us pass off as a worship service. When we put ourselves into it, though, people will put themselves into the pews. Worship is meant to be, and was always meant to be, top priority. If it is not so for us, we are very likely inappropriately out of step with our congregation's latent hunger for better worship. When we lead worship with excellence, people will soon join us in declaring worship a top-priority item.

Christian education always has a sentimental tug to it. Seeing the little children scamper forward for the children's sermon, all gussied up in their freshly pressed Sunday best outfit, is guaranteed to bring approving smiles from the congregation. Watching folks grin ear to ear when we tell them our youth fellowship has the largest attendance in years, or that our youth group is now the place to be in this town, reminds us that parishioners just love Christian education for children and youth. No wonder a scout troop and a summer program for kiddos were already priority items when I arrived at that parish I mentioned earlier. We are very unlikely to be out of step with a congregation's priorities if we put an emphasis on Christian education.

Where we can make the biggest impact in working with the church on this shared priority is by teaching an adult class. Hours spent preparing a class for adults are hours well invested. I have found that the most basic introductory Bible survey is a guaranteed winner. People flock to it. Churches get turned on when adults are learning together.

The church serves the Lord through worship, education, and mission in a context of hospitality.

Thus far we have thought together briefly about how very receptive church people are to language about serving the Lord. We have mentioned that worship and education are readily received as priority items. The challenge in worship and education is for us (a) to accept fully that these are indeed *our* personal priorities for ministry and (b) to invest our time to lead them well.

Developing a church where commitment to mission is a priority and hospitality becomes a lifestyle usually requires of us quite a lengthy bit of work with the congregation. Churches readily latch on to worship and education. The road to mission and hospitality is a bumpy and winding one. Folks have a latent desire to get there, but it takes a lot of interacting with us for it to happen. It takes a lot of insight on our part, and no small amount of rethinking our assumptions.

So for the remainder of this book, we will spend our time thinking together about hospitality, trying to get our minds around that one. Then we will visit the antithesis of hospitality, those inevitable conflicts of church life. We will discuss some things to think about that will not only give us equilibrium amid conflict but also help us turn conflict into a teachable moment. We then jump into what we can expect, if we try to take an existing church, with a history of its own, and help it make mission commitment a priority. The challenge to become a mission congregation demands a renewed commitment to the Lord at the congregation's core. We don't get there easily or without taking a controversial stand or two along the way.

First let's take a look at hospitality from four seemingly odd vantage points: numbers, administration, parking, and competition.

III   Company's Coming

Chapter 9

Numbers

*M*y first year in seminary, the chap who lived across the hall brought up all too often the fact that he was working with a parachurch youth organization. He volunteered one night a week to lead their meetings, which were held in private homes. One afternoon a week he visited the local high school to establish relationships with the kids and to invite them to the evening meeting. He was quite good at what he did, a fact that he was not shy about sharing with anyone who would listen. Brimming with pride, he burst into my room to tell me how successful the previous night's meeting had been. "You know the trouble with the denominational church?" he began. "You are too numbers-conscious. All you do is count how many kids attend. Kids don't want to be treated like numbers. They are human beings. That is why they flock to our meetings. Last night we had seventy-two kids in one living room. I bet you don't get that many at your meetings." I couldn't help but think that, for a group that is supposedly opposed to counting, he sure had a pretty precise number in his head.

On another occasion, many years later, I was chatting with a colleague in ministry. He was regaling me with statistics about how his ministry had been blessed. Membership was up by thirty-five people over the previous year. Giving was up 9 percent over the same period. The Sunday school was so crowded that they had to consider a building campaign. Evidently the children's department was up 18 percent in the past three years. He had my attention. I wanted to learn more about this church and the nature of their growth. "How is worship attendance going?" I asked. He seemed offended at such a shallow question. "Why, we don't play the numbers game at our church, and hope you don't at yours either." Obviously, worship attendance was not increasing. Numbers seemed quite fine and Godly as long as he could report good news. In those areas where he felt he had nothing to brag about, he went back on that old line that playing the numbers game is a no-no.

We ministers have a very confused relationship with numbers. One could say it is a love/hate relationship. We love them as a sign of God's blessing, and we hate them as the devil's effort to distract us.

Admittedly, your author is a numerical person. All through school my math test scores far outdistanced my verbal scores. In this section I do not ask anyone to be as compulsively numerical as I have been. I ask only that we realize that numbers are an important issue in our relationship with our church. Numbers are ignored at our own peril.

Whenever we have a physical examination, our doctor will determine our health largely by the numbers. The doctor knows that she cannot absolutize numbers or compare the relative value of patients by comparing their numbers. She would know that we could not state that three forty-year-old patients who weigh 150 pounds were therefore of equal health. Her knowledge of the individual patients would lead her to know that patient A is way overweight. "I am putting you on a crash diet immediately." Patient B is just right. "Keep up the good work." Patient C has fallen far under the desired weight, and the doctor is concerned. "I want to run some tests."

Such is the case with churches. A reason we shy away from the numbers game is that they make for unfair comparisons.

Some years ago I was the guest preacher in a church located in an area that was in the middle of a housing boom. Houses seemed literally to be popping up out of the ground. I recall hearing from the pastor's study, where I was going over my sermon, a conversation the church receptionist was having with a caller who was inquiring about the services that day. The receptionist's end of the conversation was this: "No, he's not preaching today. . . . Some guy named Galloway. . . . I've never heard of him either." Obviously, people would not be flocking to church to hear some big-name preacher. Nonetheless, when the pew cards had been tallied the pastor of the church told me that 118 families had made their first visit to the church that day. A hundred and eighteen families!! If that church received five hundred new members a year, they were doing a very poor job of retaining visitors. Another church in another environment might receive thirty new members in a year and it would mean they were doing an absolutely marvelous job of retaining and involving visitors. As with a physical examination, numbers are not for the sake of comparison. They measure our health, given our background and individual characteristics. Has our weight gone up or down? Is it too high or too low? What is our cholesterol? What are the numbers that appear on the printout from our blood work? It was a rising PSA number that tipped us off to the fact that I had better get to a urologist immediately. The numbers helped us find that I had prostate cancer, while it was still in the early stages. Had it not been for the numbers I would not have known that I was sick.

In our church, if there is not a good reason for our numbers being flat or declining, we might have an indication that there is a disease in the body. What does it mean that the number of new members is not rising and may be declining? Why is worship attendance going down? The number of kids in the youth program is down. What does that mean? Giving is flat or declining. Mission is declining in gross dollars as well as in percentage of total budget. These are numbers that signal trouble. There may be an illness in the body that we had better diagnose so we can take steps to effect a cure. The numbers tip us off to the fact that all is not well.

Maybe this is why we do not like numbers or the numbers game. We prefer denial. Just as some persons are afraid to have their annual physical, some churches prefer unexamined ministries lest they be judged and found wanting. After all, we want to feel that we are doing a fine job as is, thank you very much. We are happy the way it is. Don't ruin the comfortable spirituality of our life together by imposing cold numbers on it. Leave us alone.

The issue is hospitality. Scripture takes the act of welcoming very seriously. Our task as pastors is to look with a physician's eye at our church's numbers and diagnose whether we are a healthy fellowship that is doing all it can to be hospitable. The numbers in mainline denominations tell us we are not. Further tests are required.

1. I was speaking at a conference some years ago and offered the thought that success is not a mark of having sold out and failure is not a sign of integrity. We kicked that one around for a time. We chatted about faithful pastors and faithful churches we knew. We discovered that some faithful churches have grown, some have remained about the same, and some have declined in numbers. We also discussed specific types of pastors and congregations that we felt had a shallow theology. We agreed that experience had taught us all that some preachers of country-club theology presided over growing churches. Others served stagnant churches. Many were seeing their numbers decline. None of this seemed surprising.

What was surprising was to return to my original teaching—that success is not a mark of shallowness and failure is not a sign of integrity—and to hear participants at the conference say that this was stunningly new to them. It ran counter to everything they had been taught to believe about the church. They had assumed that the growing churches ought to be under a cloud of suspicion and churches that were declining deserved to be hailed as the real deal. Even though evidence showed clearly that some faithful churches grow to be quite large, more than a few pastors at the conference had nonetheless been clinging to the myth that such a thing could not happen. We had an "aha" moment. These pastors realized that many of them had been using numbers, all right. It was an inverse numbers game. They had been quite judgmental of growth and quite accepting of the lack of growth. Around the table that morning many pastors had a shocking new insight: A pastor and a church can have theological integrity, a prophetic mission, and preach the cost of discipleship, while at the same time seeing numbers added to their church.

Unfortunately, the notion that stagnant and shrinking churches are models of integrity allows us to avoid the call to be hospitable. "Why should we invite people? Why should we welcome them? Why should we follow up with them? We do not play the numbers game. We do not wish to be bigger." Some pastors actually live by the misguided notion that we are to do all we can to stay away from a hospitable church style, because encouraging new people to join our family might indicate we are "numbers conscious," shallow people.

2. Have we become lazy? In *The Road Less Traveled,* Scott Peck suggests that the opposite of love is laziness. One wonders if we have begun to engage in "comfort zone Christianity." A fellow pastor once asked me how soon we communicated with a person after the person visited our church. Apparently a family had visited this pastor's church for five weeks, and the question arose how many more times the family should visit before receiving a call. I was dumbfounded. Call as soon as they make one visit! Not to call a family that has visited for five weeks is just plain lazy. If possible, you call the instant a moving van starts unpacking the furniture.

I once served a congregation where at least one committee suffered from "comfort zone Christianity." In this case it was the fellowship committee. A handful of faithful souls had worked at fellowship for years. Now they were tired. One could see this in the way they served lemonade after worship on summer Sundays. A table with a large bowl of lemonade was put just outside the kitchen door for all comers to sip a cool glass. The only problem was that when people came out of the sanctuary they had to know to turn away from the traffic flow and locate an outdoor stairway that led down to a landing. One then had to know to make an odd turn and walk down a long sidewalk to the end of the education building, where one also had to know, for no apparent reason, to turn left. There in about twenty yards, under a tree and by the dumpster, stood the table and the lemonade. No visitors could possibly find it. There were no signs guiding thirsty people to a cool drink. To top it off, the committee expressed its frustration that so few people showed up for lemonade. When I asked why they didn't serve lemonade just outside the sanctuary where there was a beautiful courtyard, they looked at me as if I had told them to move a mountain. "It's easier to serve it by the kitchen."

I began to sense why that church's numbers had been declining. The lemonade was a symptom of what ailed the congregation. My leadership task was to help them rethink their life together. They needed to operate in a new way. Instead of deciding what to do on the basis of whether a task was easy or difficult, they needed to ask, "What is most hospitable? What is most inviting? What is most inclusive?" A major barrier to hospitality is the refusal to do what has to be done because we find it is difficult. Let me dare to say it. Sometimes our numbers are down because we and/or the congregation we serve are lazy.

3. Sometimes laziness is not the issue. We are an intimate fellowship in the church. We love each other. These qualities sometimes simply have to be priority over outreach and hospitality.

Let me explain what I mean. Remember that our working analogy is the Smythe family reunion. When the family gathers they want to catch up with each other and share the experiences they have in common. There is a bond that people who are not Smythes don't have. This is normal, and it is good.

What this means for the church is that sometimes the brothers and sisters in the faith quite appropriately engage in conversation that should not be interrupted by new people. Sometimes it is right for a wall of exclusion to be drawn up, so that intimate friendships can flourish and faith can grow. Charlie has just found out that he has cancer. He is sharing the news with Paul, who went through the same battle three years ago. These men should not be expected to have their conversation interrupted to glad-hand a visitor. Nor should they be told that the coffee hour is an inappropriate place to discuss a private matter. They are here. They see each other. They talk. Good for them.

If we are to respect the Smythes as family, we have to respect those precious moments of exclusivity. Just as the pastor and spouse need time alone without being interrupted, so do the members of the church family. We are the family of God, and the Smythes do not have to stop being family in order to be a hospitable fellowship.

Our task as pastors is to support the occasional need of some members to turn their backs on the visitors in our midst. That's right. You read me correctly. In fact, becoming a hospitable fellowship requires us to respect and even encourage those little pockets of exclusivity that naturally develop in families. To suggest that the congregation greet visitors at the coffee hour is never intended to mean that everyone should do it all the time. Besides, could you imagine the trauma of being pounced on by seventy-five grinning Smythes welcoming you to their church?

The hope is that at least a few people will be on the lookout for folks who seem to be alone. At one level we ask everyone to welcome visitors. At another level we recruit and train a handful of persons to be practitioners of hospitality. In the midst of clusters of people who are closed in on private conversations, a few parishioners seek out conversation with persons who appear to be new, or alone, or seem in some way lost. All that is needed is a few gracious people to make an inhospitable church hospitable.

4. The value of being a family of Smythes needs to be preserved in another matter as well: our capacity to show appreciation. We do a great disservice to our church family when we fail to appreciate the people who are volunteering their time in the church. Yes, we even need to appreciate the people who serve lemonade in a preposterous place. The move to serving lemonade in a better location was made only after time had been taken to help the fellowship committee decide for themselves to do it, a decision they could make only after we got them more volunteers to help.

We need to remind ourselves that this is family. As in any family, people are busy, often feeling overwhelmed. They give what time and effort they can. They respond to carrots of praise more than to sticks of judgment. They have learned how to work together without abusing each other, feeling that family is more important than results.

We ignore that feeling only at great risk. We would be terribly inconsistent if we made a big issue of showing hospitality for the stranger within our gates while at the same time showing little or no hospitality for our brother or sister faithfully laboring at our side.

I was recently scanning the annual report of a sister church that is not noted for living up to its potential. Their budget report indicated to me that giving has been flat in a time and place where one would have expected giving to have taken off. The stewardship committee report caught my eye. You would have thought they had won the Super Bowl. All the workers were thanked. The leaders of the campaign were thanked for their tireless efforts for the church. Just between you and me, the stewardship campaign looked to this outsider like a total flop. In most organizations it would have been given a negative evaluation, but in this family of faith the report oozed appreciation.

One of the valid reasons we do not rush to see our numbers go up is that we love and appreciate one another. May we never lose that. Yes, your numbers-conscious author is saying that. May we always realize that people are giving of their time and talent and treasure, and appreciating them is more important than the results they produce.

We dare not ever get so results-oriented that we grade our congregants on their efforts. We may feel like church-growth heroes or tough-as-nails managers if we condemn our stewardship committee for not producing a higher pledge total, but we have violated the family. We have abused a soul who tried hard to work for the church. We have lost something precious. The frantic effort to see a church grow can be at the expense of the dear people who have brought it to where it is. May we never be so arrogant or insensitive.

The role of the pastor is to join in and encourage the appreciation of those who are already leading in whatever way they are. It is to celebrate the effort given. It is to rejoice that God has called people like this together in this place. It is to come alongside and help glimpse an even larger vision for the future. It is to suggest "a very few ways where we might even improve the fine work you are now doing." It is to join in the effort to help us all take a few steps toward becoming an even more faithful fellowship.

So we rejoice in this fellowship that has come to love the cast of characters who miss a few notes in choir on Sunday, the stewardship chair who is not so good at asking for money, the youth worker who has no administrative skills, or the program leader who has a need to be in control. We are family here, and we dare not lose our sense of family.

The bottom line of this chapter is not only that hospitality is a must for the church, but that hospitality does begin at home and is felt in how we treat our own parishioners. The early church grew in no small part because the world marveled at how these Christians treated each other. Any efforts to grow a church are best done from within the existing family, not at the expense of it. Anybody who thinks this is easy is an idiot.

Chapter 10

Administration

A sage advisor in seminary hit the nail on the head when he observed that most ministers claim that what they like least about the parish ministry is administration. He went on to say that most ministers also claim that administration is where they spend most of their time.

After several decades of trying to give an objective eye to my own work and listen intently to colleagues, the seminary advisor has proven to be a prophet. I often feel buried under a mountain of "stuff" cluttering my desk and calendar. A fellow pastor just yesterday said that her ministry was stifled by all the administrative demands. "How can I carry a responsible load of counseling and make my calls when I have all this paperwork and busywork coming at me all the time?" All of us who heard her knew exactly how she felt.

Most of us were called by God to minister. Some of us heard the call to preach. Others were called to be shepherds of the flock. Others were called to teach or work for justice. More than a few of us harbored our Quixote-like illusions about saving the world, remaking the church, or at least doing some good in the name of the Lord. Almost none of us expected to spend so much of our time worrying about room arrangements, getting out mailings, meeting newsletter and bulletin deadlines, rounding up somebody to mow the church lawn, calling the people who fix the church's furnace when it conks out, making sure there are pencils in the pew racks, or trying to cover for the guy who forgets to order the offering envelopes. Elijah took on the prophets of Baal, Paul incited riots, and we pore over a catalog to see if we might be able to get a more efficient, less noisy folding machine.

Not only does administration feel to us like demeaning drudgery, it is boring. Like running the bulletin every week, it is repetitive, the same old same old with no visible sign of progress or having had any impact except to occupy the lady who feels it her God-given task to correct all our spelling and syntax bloopers every week. Her maddening habit of leaving a red-penciled bulletin in the office typifies that cadre of parishioners who like nothing better than to pop off at church meetings about what lousy administrators ministers are.

Not surprisingly, administering wears on us and poisons our attitude. If we aren't careful, we begin to resent the ministry, the congregation, and the individuals with whom we interact. We feel put upon by demands for our time. We can't figure why we are the ones who have to be sure the slide projector is up and functional, the chairs in place, and the coffee and cookies ready to serve. Even if we have delegated all of it, we sense the pressure to get it done. We start to feel like victims of people putting deadlines on us, expecting answers. "Is your article ready?" "How are you going to deal with the fact that the scouts and the afternoon circle are both signed up for the parlor at three?" "We don't have enough paper to run the bulletin." "There's a leak in the sanctuary ceiling." "Mr. Oozie dropped in to see you. He says he only needs about fifteen minutes." "The Howitzers just called. They can't lead the junior high program tonight."

We get to the point that we don't want to solve these problems. We don't want to crank out the words to meet someone else's deadline. We don't want to see whoever just dropped in. We are reacting. We begin to defend ourselves against our parishioners instead of proactively reaching out in love. We resonate to the time management gurus who tell us not to fall under the tyranny of the urgent. Know what is important and do that. Perhaps in a perfect world the guru would be right on. As we have said, in church everything has an importance. Besides, haven't we found all too often that whenever we schedule a morning to prepare a sermon the phone rings with the voice of an anxious parent whose daughter was just in a serious accident and is being taken by ambulance to the local hospital? In such a case we realize that in our calling the urgent often trumps even what we thought was our top priority.

Alas, there is more. It would be quite tolerable if the interruptions were all cases where we could feel we were doing God's work. Instead, we get the Chinese water torture of phone messages, paper, scheduling, arranging, drip, drip, drip. Coordinating, soothing hurt feelings, clarifying endless misunderstandings too often dulls our days and numbs our minds. Most of us know by frustrating experience that we clergy types like administration least, and do it most.

While your author has certainly not escaped the emotional toll of what seems like senseless menial drudgery, one insight has consistently helped me recuperate and find my calling again. Time and again I am reminded that a high percentage of what passes as administration is better recognized as the ministry of hospitality. It is when I lose sight of my role as host—or in the analogy of this book, a facilitator of a family reunion—that much of my activity loses its meaning and feels like pointless busywork.

When we begin to see ourselves as hosts and hostesses for the family of God, our whole perspective on what we do changes. Instead of being a maddening alternative to the Lord's work, our daily activity puts us very much in concert with the will of God. Few behaviors are more consistently applauded in Scripture than acts of hospitality, whether entertaining angels unawares or taking in the stranger. For all of the hot-button culture war debates over the Sodom and Gomorrah text, one thing is clear: the citizens of those towns failed to show hospitality.

Our so-called administrative work needs to be reimagined. Let's think of a dinner party. We discuss with our spouse the concept. We decide on a Friday evening three weeks hence, a night chosen because it will not wear us out on a Saturday night before having to preach, and it also happens to be a night when no wedding rehearsals are scheduled. So we agree. A dinner party it will be, on that particular night.

Now if we apply our burned-out "I hate administration" mind-set to the dinner party, and if we refuse to do the urgent so that we can concentrate on our idea of the important, our actions will become absurd. We will scrupulously avoid all demeaning administration. We will instead spend our three weeks reading as many contemporary magazines as we can, so that we can be scintillating in conversation. We can lead the group into the right topics and impress them with our knowledge. Details about arrangements will just have to take care of themselves. We won't demean ourselves by wasting time on such secondary matters.

Even to contemplate such absurdity is too farfetched to seem plausible. Obviously, once we decide on having the party, arrangements and details come to life. We have a "meeting," a "nominating committee meeting" with our spouse, to decide whom to invite. We have a "meeting" to decide how many should be invited. Should it be a large buffet or a small sit-down? Should we have a theme? The agenda takes shape. Casual or dressy? We decide small. Three couples. Casual. Invite by phone. Our spouse will phone. We clean the house. We mow the lawn and fuss with the landscaping. We plan the early evening for the living room. Drinks and hors d'oeuvres. We bring in an extra couple of chairs. Napkins. Flowers. We check the menu. We check food allergies. We shop. We cook. We set the table and light the candles. We are administrating for all we are worth, and we are energized by it because we are hosting guests in our home and we want them to have a good time. We are doing it for them, for the evening, and for our friendship. Hospitality gives purpose to housecleaning and yard work. We literally throw ourselves into it.

I am inspired to such imagery when I travel to attend a board meeting at a college or seminary. Every time the treatment is the same: excellent. They have invited me well ahead of time, so that I can clear my calendar to attend. They have taken care of accommodations. A packet of materials has been prepared, giving me exactly what I need, answering my every question. Meals are arranged to help me relax, feel included, and have a great time. At the conference table a place has been prepared, with notepad, pencil, water, and sometimes candy. I am made to feel wanted, included, and useful. The details and arrangements have been handled behind the scenes by people who have my needs in mind and who convey to me a sense that they enjoy my company. They hearken to my requests and act as if my question, which is already answered four times in the materials I have misplaced, is a very reasonable question that they are more than glad to answer. I come away exhilarated and can't wait to go back for more, because I have been exposed to hospitality, hospitality, hospitality, good old-fashioned biblical hospitality.

Imagine how our churches would come alive if we let hospitality define what we do. Arranging the chairs is not demeaning, grunt work. It is the host and hostess preparing for the guests. The church bulletin is not a dull routine. It is something to help our guests be guided in their worship, to be welcomed into the fellowship, to be invited to feel at home. Cleaning the building, if necessary painting the walls, mowing the lawn, and adding beauty to the landscaping—all are done to prepare for the party. Lining up the ushers, getting people to do child care, putting up signs so new people can easily find their way around—all to host God's celebration. Sending out minutes, brewing coffee, arranging the table, making sure the temperature and ventilation are right—all because some of God's children will be coming to God's house and we are the host and hostess. These people who are coming are so important that Jesus died for them. Jesus wants us to do everything in our power and ability to treat them royally.

At a time when many persons are leaving the parish ministry fed up with the drudgery of administration, I wonder how many of them were driven to this despair because they forgot their calling to be hospitable. The image of host has resuscitated my ministry more than once. It gives us purpose. It gives meaning and excitement to our calendar.

When the hospitality image defines our ministry we see a wonderful opportunity and reason to be alive. The Lord has invited quite a number of people to the house of God next Sunday morning. God has great plans for them on that day. The Lord has invited a smaller group Tuesday morning to study the Bible and another group Wednesday evening to discern what is God's will on some organizational matters. God wants all people to be welcomed, freed to grow, made to know they belong. Seen in this light, all the work on details and arrangements is some of the most important, exciting work we can do.

Chapter 11

Parking

I was born during the Roosevelt administration (OK, I know what you're thinking and I don't think it's very funny; I'm referring to Franklin, not Teddy). I was reared in the churchianity of the Eisenhower years, those fabulous '50s when families worshiped together. Going to church was the thing to do.

In the '50s a typical family had only one car. This is the reason why asking for the car for Friday or Saturday night was such a big deal. If we might use the TV Cleaver family from the *Leave It to Beaver* series as an example, Ward, June, Wally, and the Beaver piled into the family car and drove to church together. Four people, one car.

Today June drives to church without Ward, who is either nonreligious or worships elsewhere. Since the Beaver has a soccer game right after church and June has to stay for a brief meeting of her committee, Wally brings another family car so that he can get Beaver to his game after he has put on his uniform in the church men's room. Three people, two cars.

For a church today to bring the same number of people to worship as attended in the '50s requires more than double the number of parking spaces that we needed back when our beloved Ike was in the Oval Office.

Amazingly, many church folks still live with the illusion that this need not be the case. Denial on this one is rampant. People wonder why we can't return to the good old days.

One reason we can't go back is that the economic situation of America has changed. Families now have more than one car. Some families in suburban communities have a car for every driver in the household. With the opportunity and freedom that this affords, people will take advantage by each bringing his or her own car to church.

As we have just noted, our society has become very pluralistic. The old barriers between religions have happily been broken down. Couples marry across denominational and even across religious lines. I virtually never marry a couple anymore where both of them are members of our congregation. I rarely marry a couple where both of them are even a part of our denomination. Protestant-Catholic weddings are very common. Christian-Jewish weddings are not uncommon. These couples frequently solve the religious issue by deciding not to find a common house of worship. June attends; Ward goes elsewhere.

Any realistic planning to accommodate cars on Sunday morning has to factor in the growing number of adults who drive to church alone. Not only is Ward's nonaffiliation a factor; Ward and June may have divorced. June may be widowed. Wally and the Beaver may have adamantly refused to have anything to do with June's church, and will not come with her. June has no choice but to come alone. One car, one person.

The demographic landscape has changed dramatically, and we feel it in our parking squeeze Sunday morning. Some years ago I stood in the parking lot of the church I was then serving and watched as eight cars in a row turned in with only one person in each car. One person, one car.

Like it or not, we have lost the concept of Sabbath in our secular culture. Stores are open on Sunday, games are played, school events, charity events, and social outings are routinely scheduled on Sunday morning. People go to the office to put in a few extra hours of work. These folks need the flexibility of having different cars to transport them. If Ward is playing golf, June has to come to church without him or stay home. To assume that we can declare an old-world order in which everyone drives together in the same family car is a naïveté suggesting that one has been living under a rock. Shall we get the stores to close, the golf courses not to let anyone on before twelve-thirty P.M. on Sundays, the soccer leagues to cancel Sunday games, the corporations not to let anyone in the office on Sunday, or not allow any social events to be scheduled on the Sabbath Day? You try it. Shall we urge the people to withdraw from the pagan culture and practice a strict Sabbath observance? From time to time I preach sermons on the need to recapture the Sabbath. I have had about as much luck as I do when I urge all the people to tithe their pretax income and holdings.

Why not face reality? Our churches are located in a frantically busy world, where people have frantically busy lives and need cars to get them where they are going. They used to build houses with a detached one-car garage. Now an attached two-car garage is assumed, and many new homes have three-car garages attached to the house. We have more cars and they are more attached to our lives.

1. Our churches need to provide one parking space for every one and a half

to two persons we anticipate will be in the building at the peak time Sunday morning.

2. Suburban churches are under more pressure than urban churches to provide sufficient, highly visible off-street parking. People in our urban areas anticipate needing extra time to cope with the hassle of searching for on-street parking or an out-of-the-way lot. Suburbanites are conditioned by the mall, with sprawling parking for umpteen cars. People in the "burbs" are unpleasantly surprised by a lack of parking, get mad, and have a tendency to storm off, refusing to come to church at all.

3. A contributing reason to the stagnation and decline of mainline Protestant churches is that our churches are located in areas where the parking space that was sufficient for the '50s is woefully insufficient to meet today's demand.

4. Until we find a way to provide ample parking, our churches will stagnate.

For far too many people, that seems to be OK. Facing the parking issue, particularly in a suburban community, runs the risk of coming up against the idolatrous loyalty that persons have to the suburban ethos, which too often opposes churches' growing in their neighborhoods. Most importantly for our purposes, confronting the need for parking will reveal, sadly, that many who are members of the church seem more wedded to the suburban lifestyle than to having a vital, growing church that is serving the Lord with integrity. I have spoken with few ministers who have come out of the discussion on parking with anything but total disillusionment and despair.

On the parking issue, many suggestions will be offered, most of which are little more than wishful thinking. Carpooling is a popular idea to suggest, and in a modest way it can work, but as a solution it is close to useless. Our experience with most families is that they can barely get themselves out of bed, fed, dressed, and in any way mobilized to get to church on time as it is. Asking two such households to merge in a car-pool situation is usually out of the question. Even those who come to church alone have their own frazzled Sunday mornings.

Where the conversation gets close to the core and makes the parking debate a teachable moment is when parishioners challenge their own church with a line to the effect that if we were really committed we would not mind walking an extra distance to get here. After all, people walk a mile or more to get to a football game, and sometimes they even walk that distance in the rain. Why aren't we church people able to demonstrate that kind of commitment?

The argument is good, painfully so. It challenges us where we need to be challenged, at the level of our commitment. It hits us with the prophetic truth that many in our churches are more personally committed to getting to a football game than they are to getting to a service of worship. We need to spend some time as a congregation discussing this issue in just this light. Why aren't we a people so committed to Jesus Christ that we're willing to put up with some inconvenience and an extra long walk? For all of its rancor, the conversation raises some good questions.

The most teachable moment comes when persons say what they will inevitably say in this debate: "If a member of this church is so uncommitted that he won't walk a few extra hundred yards to worship, then we don't need him in our church. Let him join another church." To our suggestion that we need convenient parking so that visitors who are coming to our church might feel welcome and want to attend, the reply is the same. "If she won't come to a church because it is inconvenient to her, then we don't want her either."

We can all understand the frustration folks feel when people who come to church act like consumers who want to do convenience shopping. To be sure, we feel the anguish of watching people leave in droves when church life becomes the slightest bit awkward or taxing. There is something in us that wants to join in the chorus of singing, "Good riddance."

There is a problem, though. If a person on the rolls of our church demonstrates a lack of faithful discipleship by refusing to come to church when parking is unavailable, then the question is, how is that person going to become a faithful disciple? If our lack of parking turns the person away from the church and that person does not worship God or come into the presence of teaching about Jesus Christ, then we have put a barrier between that person and spiritual growth. We cannot ask the uncommitted to act and behave as if they were committed. They will consistently demonstrate their lack of commitment. It is for us in leadership positions in the church to remove barriers, to open doors, and to invite in the noncommitted so that the Holy Spirit can move and the uncommitted can become committed. The debate over the parking issue can remind us as a church that we have a ministry of evangelism even to those uncommitted folks who are on the rolls of the church.

None of us would be so dull-witted as to suppose that a person must be a fully dedicated Christian before that person is allowed to attend our church for the first time. All of us would realize that our call is to reach out to the community, to engage those persons who have not yet become disciples. The parking debate often calls the question as to whether we are serious about the tasks of evangelism and hospitality. Should we not be hoping that persons who have absolutely no dedication to the cause of Christ will come to the church on Sunday morning? Should we not be hoping that persons with no willingness to go the extra mile will come to the church? Should we not be hoping that we will be reaching out to those persons whose lives have not yet been changed? Isn't this what evangelism is all about? Isn't this one of our major reasons for existing?

When we think about those persons driving out of the parking lot because there was no place to park, we need to be sensitive to the dynamic that is going on within that car. That was the day a couple decided to "try" our church, and their trying may have been the result of her praying for fifteen years that he would finally say, "Let's go to church together." Well, now the opportunity has been lost. Or perhaps a person was grasping at a straw, willing to try anything to find direction in a desperate life. But it didn't take much to get that person to turn away, because desperation lives at the door of escape. Or, at the risk of being melodramatic, maybe in the car was a person living his or her last Sunday on this earth, having the last chance to hear the gospel message.

Are we really intending to say that if a person cannot find a parking space and drives away in disgust that this is the kind of person we don't want or need? Is the message that our church conveys that we don't care if nondisciples become disciples? Are we saying that if you are not committed, we do not want you? Is this our mantra of evangelism and hospitality?

Sad to say, that seems to be exactly where many in the church are, and the parking-lot debate is an arena where our spiritual bankruptcy in evangelism and hospitality is most readily exposed. The debate will reveal that many in the church do not have much interest in welcoming new non-Christians and helping them become Christians. It will reveal that the church does not really put much of an effort into enabling persons to grow in their discipleship. It will expose that the church does not seem to think that it makes much of a difference whether folks attend or do not. It will expose that we do not believe we have anything to offer a hurting world, at least not enough to make an effort to get people to come and see what it is that we do have. In the parking debate, too many church folk declare that they have little interest in reaching out to the world.

Admittedly, these are deliberately harsh words. Because I have had more than my share of parking discussions, I am convinced that the debates reveal our shallow cultural idolatry. It is a disillusioning debate. Let's not let our disillusionment hold us back. We have an obligation to help our church see how we can be a more hospitable witness to Jesus.

1. We can share images with our congregation, imagining who those people are who drive away. They are not bad people. They are needy people, just as we are. We can pray for that searching soul who is not yet dedicated enough to handle the inconvenience of not finding a place to park. We can reimagine the person, not as an angry ogre and shallow pagan, but as a human being who

needs to hear about Jesus. God calls us to reach out to people like this. We can begin to raise the consciousness of our people for evangelism. In teachable moments we humanize humans.

2. We can talk about being gracious hosts. We can point out that in Scripture hospitality is the lifestyle of the early church. We can talk about the folks who built the ramp two years ago at our church so that a barrier to persons in wheelchairs would be removed. Now we can begin to talk about removing the barriers that would keep the spiritually tentative from our doors. Our call is to be welcoming hosts. Scripture demands nothing less. We can challenge our people with a question like this: Have you ever hosted a large function or been invited to attend one at a family's home? Did the invitation say where to park? Did the hosts plan for extra parking? Did they provide valet service? As a rule, when a large gathering is planned in a private home, providing parking is part of hosting. Why are we not gracious hosts at church?

3. We can begin to turn over in our minds William Temple's great insight that the church exists for those who are not yet in the church.

4. We can tell our staff and officers that they should not park in the church lot if we have one, or in the closest lots if we have several. We can tell them that, by virtue of their being leaders, they are expected to show extra commitment and thus to park as far away from the church as possible. We can even make it a little bit of a joke with them that the closer they are to Jesus the farther they are expected to be parking from the sanctuary.

5. We can consider a shuttle service for staff, officers, and any who would be willing.

6. We can block off and mark not only handicapped access spaces, but spaces designated for visitors.

An ongoing discussion of parking can help an apathetic, ingrown congregation see its face in the mirror. If we are lucky, it may even turn that congregation into an open, hospitable fellowship that feels compassion for the spiritually hungry and wants to remove every barrier in the way of those who want to worship God and grow in discipleship.

Chapter 12

What's Your Competition?

I have heard this question quite often over the years. "What's your competition?" It typifies the consumer mind-set that counts church members in terms of market share, and sizes up other congregations as worthy or unworthy competitors in a dog-eat-dog marketplace. The Presbyterian pastor still winces when reminded of the young couple who visited for three weeks but joined the Baptist church because they liked the Friday square dancing. The Episcopalians recall the forty-year-old divorcee who left their church because the Methodists had a better singles group. Then there's the family that came to us from a neighboring church of our denomination because our music is so good. We all too easily slip into the guise of department-store owners trying to woo and keep customers by upgrading our products and improving our service. Many among us live in fear that an independent St. Wal-Marts will build a megachurch, with something for everybody and plenty of parking, that will threaten to put us out of business.

So stormy is the debate about church growth techniques that one cannot even mention market shares and competition without hopelessly dividing the house. No doubt our first paragraph drew either suspicion or hostility from readers who are dead set against the church growth movement, believe competition is ungodly, and want nothing to do with any pastor who even hints at such things. They remind us that all around us is competition. Sports increasingly dominate public interest, the media, and casual conversation. The moods of cities rise and fall with the fortunes of their professional sports teams. Our economy is founded on competition. Our politics are all about competition. Our children are in uniforms competing while they still have their baby teeth. Isn't the church supposed to show a more excellent way? These colleagues of ours are a prophetic voice calling us to be a counterculture in the church. The church is to be a haven, where people can come to get away from the cutthroat world and live in wholesome community. These colleagues make clear they want no part of competition.

On the other hand, we hear from alert, progressive colleagues who wish the church would wake up to the possibilities for reaching people in new and creative ways. Why not have a business plan with a vision statement? Why not discover what the unchurched of our community want and need? Why not target certain demographic segments of the parish with a ministry specially tailored to their needs? Why not advertise? Why not be user-friendly, service oriented, customer driven? Our call is to reach people for Christ. Why are we not using the best techniques available for reaching people? Why not then quantify our results to see how we are doing?

So how do we carry on a ministry with integrity in this highly competitive culture? Is competition good or bad? How do we deal with competitive urges within ourselves? What do we say in answer to the innocently intended question "What's your competition?"

The thesis of this chapter is that competition is an inevitable part of church life. Because we are so viscerally divided on the subject of competing, we have a very difficult time discussing it, or even recognizing it or admitting it. Sadly, on few subjects are we less honest or less consistent.

What follows are some jottings to help us recognize and fess up to the competitive spirit within our fellowship, to note some of its helpful dynamics, and to note where it can be destructive, especially when we mistakenly see other congregations as our competition. Finally, we will hold up some examples of how competition can actually be a God-given insight into our calling.

Rarely are we clergy more hilarious than in the convoluted way "the reverends" compete. We posture our way through an awkward fumbling act to look humble and disinterested while frantically scheming to win. The whole charade is based on deception. In fact, it borders on ludicrous dishonesty.

Understand the rules of the game: We have been schooled to know that it is gauche to suggest we actually want to beat our fellow candidates and be elected to a denominational honor, or to outdistance the field and be called to a bigger church. So politicking, clergy style, is required. We must disavow any personal interest in the position that is up for grabs. We must shun all language that even hints at a competitive spirit or attempting to elevate our own position for our own sake.

When we feel desperate to get out of our present ministry at a church that is driving us batty, we cannot admit it. A friend will call and ask us how we are doing. Would we be open to a move? We say, "I love it here, but I would be open to consider another church, if the Holy Spirit wants me there." We sound religious, while lying through our teeth. What we really mean is, "I hate this place! Get me out of here! I'll go anywhere! Please help me. I'm desperate."

I wound up in a buffet line once with a man who had been nominated for the office of Moderator of our denomination. In conversation I mentioned his candidacy. Immediately he assured me that he had not sought the office and really wasn't sure that he wanted it. Putting on his solemn-servant look, he told me he had a responsibility to be open to the Lord if the Lord wanted him to be Moderator. Sounded perfect. Wasn't true. When he lost the election, the poor chap was devastated.

What an odd ritual! We compete by trying to make it look as if we aren't competing. We show that we want to move by saying we don't want to move. We assume the image of a humble servant awaiting the Lord's lead, all the while having strategy session after strategy session to figure out how we can avoid looking as if we want to win this thing, a charade that enhances our chances of winning this thing.

Why not be honest? Why not begin the discussion by admitting we are human? We like to win more than we like to lose. We like to be given honor and authority. If nominated, we like to be elected; if considered, we like to be called. Why can't we cut the hypocritical gibberish and admit, if only to ourselves, that there is a good deal of competitive feeling within us and within our churches?

When we listen to the voice of our congregation, we will hear the words of a people schooled in a competitive culture. They like to win and they want their church to be a winner. They fret when statistical reports indicate we are not doing well vis-à-vis other churches. They rejoice when we are.

One search committee admitted they invited me to be their pastor in no small part so that I could go into direct competition with a pastor not far from them who was building a megachurch. I didn't go, though I admit to being intrigued by the competitive challenge.

Some communities have a three-hour Good Friday service, with different pastors each preaching on one of the seven last words of Jesus. It is not uncommon for at least a handful of church attendees that day to give each preacher a score and discuss the results after the service. "The Methodist was number one. The Lutheran was second." I once publicly referred to the service as a "Pillsbury preach-off." People were offended. It evidently cost me points on some score cards in that year's preach-off.

Competition is in the air we breathe. A parishioner calls me aside to voice concern that two families have just transferred membership to a neighboring church. "We don't want that church to get ahead of us, you know." A staff member notes with alarm that the church down the street seems to have more cars than we do on Sundays. Someone brags, "We have the best youth program in town. Our church is the hot church now." We get a call informing us that "the Episcopal church just took more people than we did on their mission trip."

When asked "What is your competition?" many of our parishioners would have a ready answer. They would list the neighboring congregations, rate their relative strengths and weaknesses, position them on the theological spectrum, and then declare how our church stacks up in the competition for market share. It is how many folks think. Hey, be honest. It's how we have been known to think too.

This is not all bad. I have also found that the Lord sometimes uses unlikely characters to energize us. The church that is deviously seducing our members may represent God's way of teaching us something. No doubt that church is doing some things extraordinarily well. Why not learn from them? A creative use of competitive juices can spur us to the higher level of excellence we should have been seeking all along. Such competition is uncomfortable for us because it destroys our laziness. It jars us out of complacency. Thank God for competition that makes us better!

Sometimes we knock competition because it is so blatantly manipulative, like the denominational leaders who list churches according to who is doing the most in mission. Mind you, they are fair about it. So that big churches don't have unfair advantage, the lists are usually arranged in per capita terms. The listing obviously has a manipulative intent of getting more mission money. But, so what? Such lists remind us what is possible. Yes, it's competition, but we should see these lists as an eye-opener, to do better. In many ways other churches serve to call us to take the next step up toward becoming the fellowship the Lord intends us to be.

I admit that while competitive thinking can be oxygen for our ministries, it can also be toxic, especially if misdirected. For all we can gain from being spurred on by other churches, we must remember that the answer to the question "What is your competition?" is not supposed to be those other churches. Two events in my ministry have helped me not only to believe this truth with my head, but to know it in my bank of personal experience. Early in my ministry, word came to me that the hottest youth program in town was an ecumenical venture meeting once a month and bringing together quite large groups from the local Roman Catholic and Episcopal churches. Our own fellowship was growing in numbers but paled in comparison to the literally hundreds of kids that were flocking to this extravaganza, which combined a brief religious program with an extended dance and a live rock band. As pressure mounted from parishioners for us to keep up with other churches, I went along. Once a month our group joined their group in one great big happy megagroup. For a time I admit to being seduced by the heady world of gathering five or six hundred teenagers in one place. Then I noted that the other weeks our fellowship numbers were slipping. Our momentum was broken; our continuity was lost. We paid a price.

Then and there I had an insight. All that really matters is whether our group is faithfully serving the Lord. Are we practicing faithful hospitality? Are we bringing new people to the Lord? Are we on the right track? It does not matter if the church down the street is drawing a zillion people every time it opens its doors. What matters is whether we are healthy and, I dare to add, whether we are growing.

The second experience is more recent. The church I serve in suburban Philadelphia is quite close to the King of Prussia Mall, a gargantuan, sprawling minicity with parking for a fair percentage of the Commonwealth of Pennsylvania. A year or so into my tenure here I ventured toward the mall one day between Thanksgiving and New Year's. My mistake. First, you can't get through the gridlock. Then you can't park in the same zip code as the store you want to visit. I spent a long time on a short trip.

My long day's journey into shopping did offer an epiphany. It occurred to me, looking out at an endless sea of cars owned by people who obviously lived within driving distance of our parish, that if every church in the area maxed out its building with multiple services they could not possibly reach all the people on the roads and at the mall during the Christmas season. It makes absolutely no difference how well other churches do. There will always be more than enough people left for our congregation to reach and involve.

Read my font: Our competition is not other churches. We are on the same side.

Paul writes:

Finally, be strong in the Lord and in the strength of [the Lord's] power. Put on the whole armor of God, so that you may be able to stand against the wiles of the devil. For our struggle is not against enemies of blood and flesh, but against the rulers, against the authorities, against the cosmic powers of this present darkness, against the spiritual forces of evil in the heavenly places. Therefore take up the whole armor of God, so that you may be able to withstand on that evil day, and having done everything, to stand firm. Stand therefore, and fasten the belt of truth around your waist, and put on the breastplate of righteousness. As shoes for your feet put on whatever will make you ready to proclaim the gospel of peace. With all of these, take the shield of faith, with which you will be able to quench all the flaming arrows of the evil one. Take the helmet of salvation, and the sword of the Spirit, which is the word of God. (Eph. 6:10–17)

As we read Scripture, the problem is clearly not with competition per se. The problem is that we compete with the wrong opponent. Instead of competing with other congregations, we should see ourselves as standing with other congregations in competition with the real opponent: the rulers . . . the authorities . . . the cosmic powers . . . the spiritual forces of evil.

To be candid, we have a hard time gearing up for battle because we are a house divided on what "the spiritual forces of evil" are. Are "the cosmic powers" pro-life or pro-choice? Are "the authorities" for or against gay ordination? Is the real issue pornography or racism? At the outset of the twenty-first century we are not a united army taking on the powers of evil. We exhaust our energy in intramural skirmishes. So to answer the question "What is your competition?" is not easy.

Let's at least raise one last thought on which one hopes we can all agree. When asked the question "What is your competition?" my first instinct is to say that I am. I often think that the biggest barrier to our church's becoming all the Lord hopes it will be is me. My mind is limited. My energy runs out. I make mistakes in prioritizing time. Ministry is a constant competition against the lesser parts of my own nature, as I try to become more faithful, more competent, more able to pastor. I compete against "the spiritual forces of evil" within myself and I call the congregation to battle "the cosmic powers" that hurt our life together.

The competition we face in leading a congregation is the lethargy and cultural conformity that has captured us and too many of our parishioners. We are like the cartoon character Pogo: "We have met the enemy and it is us." Our lack of commitment, our collective failure to be creative, our busy lives eaten up by ungodly pursuits are the real competition. We see it in our lazy habit of withholding hospitality. That's how the spiritual forces of evil get us. Even surrounded by a self-absorbed materialistic culture, and being neighbors to strong, vital congregations, the answer to the question "What is your competition?" boils down to a simple answer. "We are."

As we shall see, nowhere does our competition with ourselves leave us in worse shape than do the inevitable conflicts that constantly chew up our own congregations.

IV

Conflict Happens

Chapter 13

Conflict

On practically every brochure table and church bulletin board is material announcing yet another conflict management seminar. Books are written about it. Management gurus help us figure out how to use our pulpits, our classrooms, our counseling, our scheduling, all in service to managing conflict. Obviously, there is a market for these publications and seminars.

Like competition, and in some ways because of it, conflict is an inevitable reality in our churches. I have not yet seen a book or seminar entitled "How to get all conflict out of your church." No one would be so naive as to think conflict could be eliminated. In fact, anyone with intimate experience with the parish might be tempted to rephrase Jesus' teaching: "Where two or three are gathered together in my name, you have two or three opinions and a conflict."

Even a cursory reading of Scripture would tell us conflict was typical in the early church. Jesus' disciples had spats, rivalries, and conflicts with each other. Jesus had conflicts with the disciples. Peter and Paul had at it. Paul read the riot act to the Galatians. Paul had to write to the Corinthians and tell them to quit warring with each other. Paul wrote to Timothy about how to handle a curriculum squabble. The list goes on and on. To be a part of the early church was to be a part of an organization that elevated conflict to an art form. Why should it be any different for us in the church today?

Our purpose in this section is not to give a distillation of conflict management techniques. The experts in the field have their valid place. I leave it to the reader to pick up a book or attend a seminar on the subject. Helpful insight is there.

Our purpose is to bring to mind a concept of the church, a style of ministry, an increased ability to recognize what is going on right before our eyes as the congregation works its way through one donnybrook after another. On these pages we try to note why certain things happen. We try to suggest ways we can be more pastoral and/or prophetic while the bombs are bursting in air.

Let's begin by naming conflict. It is competition for space. In its ultimate form—war—military strategists sit in the war room peering at a map of the battle area. Certain space is in the hands of the enemy. Certain space is ours. By moving the tanks over here and bombing there, we should be able to take a chunk of their space for ourselves. Eventually we hope they surrender and we have control of all their space, thus winning the battle area for truth, justice, and the American way.

Another example is football. As we do in war, we dress up in uniforms, and take the field of battle as the offense or the defense. The defense blitzes. The offense throws bombs. While the object is to score more points than the other team, coaches tell us it is all about field position. Statisticians keep a tally of yards gained or given up. We wonder if the ball is in our territory or theirs. The game is played out trying to move into space occupied by the other team and to keep the other team from marching into our space. Conflict is competition for space.

Not surprisingly, a basic conflict within many congregations could best be described as a "turf war." The Christian education committee feels that the mission committee has come onto its turf by scheduling a mission awareness class. "If it's a class, it's education," they protest. The choir feels as though the worship committee has invaded its turf by calling for more modern music. In one church I served, two women each thought the chancel flowers were her individual domain. When one week the other woman changed the flowers the first woman had arranged . . . well, you can imagine.

All of this is to say that people think they have certain turf staked out. Sometimes it's organizational. Folks want to have a stake in what the congregation is doing, have a place at the table. They are trying to be responsible church people, and they can quite easily be hurt. It does not take much to make a soul feel homeless within the congregation. I think of the man who was asked to draw up a proposal for expanding the church's mission by initiating a dialogue with a congregation in the third world. He worked hard, and had the report almost ready for presentation when the mission committee got excited about a ministry in a nearby city. They voted to put aside the third-world church dialogue for now. The chap who had worked so hard felt shunned by the committee, put down. He felt judged by their decision. He wondered why they shoved him off the mission turf without even hearing his report. He felt devalued.

The space battles are not restricted to skirmishes within our organizational chart. Sometimes the fight is simply over space itself. Who gets the fellowship hall the second Sunday evening of next month? The youth group usually has it, but the women have scheduled a speaker, and the number of people registered to show up demands the fellowship hall because it is the only room big enough to hold everyone. How could we have forgotten? That is the night of the annual scout banquet. Three groups—one room. Two groups will feel like "second-class citizens around here" as a result of whatever we decide.

We have developed a "Blue Book." It was the "Red Book" in my last parish. This book has a page for every day of the year. Each page is blocked out morning, afternoon, and evening. Only the church secretary or secretaries are allowed to write in the book, which is the bible of space use. A secretary might have written in that the scouts have their annual dinner in the fellowship hall. She would initial the entry and date it. When the youth group plans its program, they will note that the scouts have this night reserved. The youth will then plan around it. The women will note that there is a limit to how many persons can attend their program because the fellowship hall is taken. First come, first served in the "Blue Book."

It is a wonderful theory. When it works, we rejoice. You know how it is. The Boy Scouts forget to tell us the exact date of their banquet until after they have already sent out the invitations. The youth group assumes they have the room every week, so they forget to sign up. The women had been signed up for the smaller parlor. Now realizing they anticipate such a large attendance and thinking the fellowship hall is available, they plan to move their program there, but don't tell anyone. By the time the mess hits my desk, I'm ready to head for cover.

Looking at competition for space another way, there is only so much room on the church's agenda. We only have so much time and energy. If the social ministry folks seem to have taken the hill, is there a priority place on the agenda for the evangelism group? It is not uncommon for a pastor to be approached by parishioners who are concerned that "the right wingers are trying to take over this church." Or "It seems the liberals control everything that happens around here." Or "Our music program has taken over everything. They act like they are God. They get everything they want." There are only so many front burners in any congregation. In various ways all the different interest groups in the church try to crowd themselves onto those burners, even if it means pushing other interests to the back burners for a while.

The battle for the church's agenda is probably the most serious struggle we face in our congregations. Visitors to our church want to know if we are traditional or contemporary or blended. What role does the Bible play? Are we conservative or liberal on the issues of the day? Do we tolerate diversity, or do we not?

While visitors are looking us over, parishioners are pressing to make sure we do not tolerate certain beliefs, or conversely that we do not become intolerant.

People become conditional in their membership. "If this church is going to drift to the right, we'll look elsewhere." "If the pastor is softening the stand on gay ordination, I'm out of here." Conditional membership combined with the corollary effort by some folks to drive out of the church anyone who does not agree with them makes the battle for space on the church's agenda quite nasty.

The struggle for space also occurs when we decide to hire staff. Since I have not yet had the opportunity to serve a church that has more annual income than we know what to do with, I've always been saddled with a parish that has to set priorities. Our income will not allow us to do all we want, hire everyone we want, do everything we want to the building, or develop all the programs we want. What do we do when the worship committee wants to increase staffing in music, the Christian education committee wants to hire someone to work with the teenagers, the mission committee wants to bring in someone to help coordinate our ministry to the urban area, the trustees want more custodial help, the personnel committee feels that we need more hours of secretarial support, and we have only enough money to hire someone twenty more hours a week? We have a conflict.

Typically, competition for space is also felt in battles for publicity. The front page of the newsletter is only so large. The poor soul who does the layout finds it not uncommon to receive a full page—"Must be on the front page"—blurb from the mission folks, another from the Christian ed people, yet another from the choir, another from the library coordinator, yet another from the women's group, something from the men's association, and still another from the singles group. Newsletter editors quit a lot.

And pulpit announcements. Some ministers do not do them. I do, and I pay the price. Everyone wants time (space) in the service for a presentation. A typical week sees three groups demanding time to trot someone to the microphone to do a "minute for thus and such." If they don't get their own "minute for thus and such," they want me to "hit it hard this week" in my announcements. They hand me notes as I enter the sanctuary—a practice I discourage—insisting, "This is an emergency." If I don't give them their space, they feel I don't care.

Bulletin boards. There are never enough. No matter how many bulletin boards we have, anyone can tell instantly which are the top locations. Even then, there are still the more aggressive groups that use masking tape to post their announcements on any old wall any time and then throw fits if their things are taken down. Or they go easel on us, putting up an easel with a poster, often situated so as to block people from entering the sanctuary.

The battle for space would be hilarious if it weren't for extremely high emotional and personal stakes. People are struggling to do well, to be recognized, to be included, to know that they and their programs are wanted. They want people to attend their program, and they want the experience to be good. Theirs is always a battle to be taken seriously.

One last area of conflict is the pastor's schedule. Even the superenergetic among us have only so much space on the calendar. We often have to practice what the medical profession calls triage to determine which persons need us most right now. Do we race to the hospital to see the person who we just learned is on the way there in an ambulance with a suspected heart attack? Or do we keep our regularly scheduled meeting with a potentially suicidal parishioner? Or do we work on the sermon forty-five hours before delivery and presently in dreadful condition?

As if the calendar were not squeezed enough, let me name three character types who are prevalent around churches these days, who throw everything out of balance by demanding time, often unrealistically and at the expense of all else on our calendars.

The first character is the "chronically desperate person" (CDP). This poor soul is simply overwhelmed by life, by health concerns, by money management, by work, by relationships. CDP is desperate for someone to come into his or her life and help straighten it out. Usually though not always single, CDP comes to church to find help and companionship. Experience will teach the congregation that it can do everything imaginable for CDP and at the end of a decade we still have CDP. Over decades CDP never changes. A new pastor will be cornered by CDP within the first week. Without limits being set, CDP will require two hours of clergy time every day until the Lord returns. After church, at fellowship suppers, at various meetings, CDP will latch onto "minister person's" (MP's) surrogate and not let go.

The second character is more dangerous, and has a high probability of leaving the church disgruntled before too long. This is the "close personal friend of the former pastor" (CPFFP). The CPFFP misses the former pastor terribly, does not believe anyone can replace the former pastor, and at the same time expects to recapture instantly the close friendship with us that the CPFFP had with the former pastor. It does not work. We cannot recapture the relationship this person had with his or her pastor, nor can we be expected to spend the time socially, spiritually, and professionally that the CPFFP spent with our predecessor. Since the CPFFP is a respected church leader, largely because of the close personal friendship with the former pastor, the CPFFP will be an expert analyst in the eyes of the congregation as to whether we are worthy to fill the loafers once worn by our sainted predecessor. No matter how we adjust our calendar to give this person space, experience says we have an inevitable saboteur who will express his or her disappointment with us in ways we hope will be nondestructive.

The final competitor for calendar space is the "retired guy" (RG), or in more extreme form the "early retired guy" (ERG). RG and his more energetic sidekick ERG are used to having an office, people saluting, importance, a reason for living. RG and ERG are used to running things. About the time his spouse is ready to admit herself to the funny farm because she can't cope with his obnoxious insistence that she let him put her life into his computer so that he can help her live more efficiently, he turns in our direction with his limitless time and as yet unfocused need for leading someone or something. We cannot prepare for these "unscheduled conferences" because in the old office RG/ERG managed by walking around, dropping in on unsuspecting subordinates. Our secretary buzzes to announce "RG is here and he says he only needs forty-five minutes of your time." Since we are under time pressure already, RG/ERG's arrival makes our heart sink. The fact that he has with him an unrequested thirty-page printout, which is a proposal to overhaul some area of the church's life that does not need overhauling, only makes our heart sink lower. The fact that he wants "on his desk" tomorrow our detailed response, so "we can get to work on it," brings our heart to near cardiac arrest. Our task is then tactfully to say we don't have time, the area does not need to be overhauled, and we greatly respect RG/ERG nonetheless. Do our parishioners have any idea how little fun we're having here?

These are but three characters from a cast of characters who want disproportionate space on our calendars. They typify, perhaps, in a lighter vein the fact that conflict happens to us all—conflict which is competition for space.

Handling it all is never easy, nor is it done without taking a toll on us who try to lead. In chapter 16 we will discuss some specific thoughts to bear in mind when we are in the midst of the stress that eats at us amid conflict. First are some further reflections on what conflict is and how it happens. The purpose of those pages will be to attempt the delicate task of easing our guilt, increasing our peace, and bolstering our courage when conflict occurs.

Chapter 14

The Tyranny of the Touchy

*B*ack in chapter 1 we met Aunt Bessie, whose potato salad had the unfortunate tendency to double folks over with cramps. We also met Uncle Fred, the man who got all the kiddos to play the same game at every reunion, boring the poor youngsters to tears. Our point in introducing these two pillars of the Smythe clan was to remind ourselves not to go barging into the reunion and depose Bessie and Fred. The family has learned to assimilate both of them into the fold. The Smythes know the downside of each and have learned to adjust and cope year after year. Bessie and Fred are family. They are fixtures. We do not threaten those two without disrupting the whole fabric of Smythe life. Even if we have a foolproof recipe for making nontoxic potato salad, and know the perfect games to make the kids happy, we should be very cautious with any suggestions. It's family business. Leave it alone.

Any of us who have had experience with the good saints at whatever our St. Smythes' may have been, know that there is another dynamic at work here. Bessie and Fred almost certainly have personal quirks about them that give them unusual power. We can feel it in our bones. If our pastoral radar is functional, we see the warning light telling us not to mess with these people.

For all the love and hugs Bessie gives the family, when it comes to that potato salad she is tough. Never does she come to a planning meeting with a genuinely objective, open mind about the menu. The potato salad is not fair game for conversation. Never does she honestly volunteer not to do her infamous dish. Should even a hint of not including the salad be mistakenly murmured under someone's breath, Aunt Bessie will give an Oscar-winning performance of how, if people don't recognize her long hours of work and don't appreciate how hard she is trying to help, then maybe it is time for her not to prepare her great-grandmother's favorite recipe and just go off and die. She inevitably equates even the remotest possibility of not having potato salad with a judgment of her as a person. She lets us know that not having her mound of cholesterol on the table is akin to telling her she is no longer wanted at the reunion. It just breaks her poor old heart not to be loved by the family she loves so much, without whom she will keel over dead. In a nutshell, Aunt Bessie has learned to get and keep power by being touchy.

It is the same story with Uncle Fred. Everyone knows that Uncle Fred lives for those games of his. We know it because he tells us. We can see it on his face if anyone voices a discouraging word in the evaluation time about other games being better. Now, beware. Fred has a temper on him. You question his games and he blows a gasket. He'll accuse you of being an atheist, of not really being a Smythe, of hating children and fun. He'll rally his cronies to turn on you. The cost of getting Fred riled up just isn't worth it. His touchiness is a force.

Essentially, touchy people are those personalities who, whether by devious design or for reasons beyond their control, have very thin skins. It takes very little discomfort to touch off an episode. With them we are not just talking about being hurt. We all get hurt. With them it is the histrionics of pain that will bring all discussion to a screeching halt. It is not just about their being angry. Who doesn't get angry at church now and then? For touchy people it is the outburst, the show of anger, the license their angry outbursts seem to give them to be verbally abusive and manipulative. People just shut down in the presence of touchy people.

In this chapter we are more likely to name the demons than to exorcise them. When it comes to the touchy, their name is legion.

The most benign is the high maintenance person who needs both lots of "face time" with the pastor and an exhaustive amount of compliments. While we want to show gratitude to all who deserve it, high-maintenance touchy types can't get enough of it. The church secretary will tip us off: "Be sure to thank So-and-so." "What did So-and-so do?" "Nothing. That doesn't matter. Say 'thank you' anyway."

In a church long ago we had a parishioner who took quite seriously the choosing of her annual Christmas card. She would send it out and then wait for the kudos to roll in. An early mistake in my ministry occurred when she closed in on me at the coffee hour, interrupted a conversation, asked if I got her Christmas card, and then just stood there. Stupid me. I said "Yea, I got it. Thanks." She acted as if I had poured hot coffee on her neatly permed blue hair.

A sage friend of hers took me aside and advised me that this woman needed extra compliments about "the card." So the next year I got to her before she could get to me. "O, my dear, you outdid yourself this year. I didn't think you could top last year's winner. This year you found it. You found the card of cards. What a sensitive, creative person you are to have found the perfect card! How did you do it?" I felt cheap, but it worked. She seemed pacified for the time being. Then I discovered that my outpouring of sugar set me up for her centerpieces at church socials, her poster for a mission project, her new hat. I soon ran out of superlatives and luckily accepted a call elsewhere.

If high-maintenance touchy people are wearisomely time-consuming but benign, others have more uncontrollable impact on the life of the congregation. They realize that a congregation is run by formal and informal authority. For example, an honest detailed organizational chart might show the men's Bible class with an arrow of accountability to the Christian education committee, which has an arrow to the ruling board. But to be complete, the chart also must have an arrow from the men's Bible class pointing to Dave, who is then accountable to no one. Dave is not an officer in the class, nor does he sit in on their planning meetings. My man Dave is a piece of work. He needs to be consulted on all Bible-class issues because if he isn't in on it, he'll call his golfing buddies who make up half the class and get them to raise you know what. Dave doesn't want to lead the class. If the leader does not share Dave's theology, Dave will be in our office asking if this church is selling its soul to the devil. All matters regarding the men's Bible class are discussed with the implicit understanding that Dave has to be kept happy. Dave is touchy. Dave has informal, but very real, power.

So we have an organizational chart with not only bureaucratic lines of authority; it also has other lines randomly pointing to individuals who have come to play a disproportionately strong role in the church. They do not necessarily have a place on the normal boards and committees, but everyone in the church family knows that these individuals have to be kept happy for the peace and unity of the church.

This is what I call "the tyranny of the touchy." They easily become tyrants, because the family has decided that it is easier to work around its touchy siblings. In fact, it is easier to acquiesce to their wishes than to go through the trauma of setting them off. When someone does say or do something to upset a touchy person, the congregation will blame the instigator for being naive and not having the best interests of the family at heart. When we pastors trigger an outburst, folks wonder about our competence. They rather wish we would just stay out of the church's life if we are going to cause all this turmoil.

Let's dissect the power of touchy people with an eye toward better understanding them. They are, after all, in the family. Certainly some of their power exists for dubious reasons. We also have to admit that they have power for reasons that are quite legitimate. Our task is to differentiate between the dubious and the legit. Then, hopefully, we can take strides to include our touchy members in the family in a fruitful way.

One observation is that touchy people use explosive words. Our society now gives added credence to anyone who claims the "O" words. All a person need do is exclaim, "I am offended," or "I am outraged," and the person has the upper hand. By claiming to be offended, these people are declaring that whoever offended them is an insensitive buffoon. By implication the church is a seedbed of insensitivity and buffoonery. The pastor is either the insensitive buffoon or knowingly permits insensitive buffoons to offend the innocent. "The church is supposed to help me find peace. I am offended. Therefore, I need your help against this church, which has not treated me as I am supposed to be treated."

When a person declares, "I am outraged," that person claims the high ground of prophetic insight. This second "O" word implies that certain behavior is outrageously inappropriate for persons following Jesus. To drop the second "O" word is tantamount to saying, "I am a person following Jesus and you are not. I am sensitive enough to God's will that my righteous indignation boils over at your careless words or deeds."

No church wants to be considered what either "O" word implies. No one ever dare question the user of the "O" words. After all, who are we to question what a person claims to feel, especially when he or she feels it so passionately? So, naturally, folks immediately side with the "O" word person in the cause of standing against whatever or whoever has offended or outraged them. Touchy people can drop an "O" bomb and bring a church to its knees.

Further, touchy people have an uncanny gift for communicating their emotions. Some of them are quite good at putting words together. Almost all of them speak with such emotional involvement that we get hooked by what they are saying. We feel the hurt with them. We feel anger toward whatever group or individual has troubled them. Touchy people seem to have a knack for pushing all the right buttons to elicit irrational support and guilt. Heaven protect the offending party from the posse rounded up by the touchy victim, for they will walk on hot coals for dear old So-and-so, "who has been so savagely treated by this heartless church." One does not easily argue against such emotion.

Having said all this, we do have to acknowledge that some of the touchy person's power has been well earned. We should know that anyone who has accumulated power in the congregation by virtue of being touchy has almost assuredly demonstrated a deep commitment to the church. Think about it. This easily hurt person has no doubt been hurt several times in the past. More than likely there have been episodes that triggered threats to quit the church.

Perhaps there have even been short times of dropping out, clear signals to the family that "this pain is more than I can bear." Yet, obviously, the person is still with us. Evidently, our touchy friend has demonstrated in the past that "this church is just too important for me to leave. I'll stay, in spite of how much I have been hurt or how angry I have been." Touchy people who did not have such a devotion to the fellowship are now doing their thing in other churches. The ones still with us have shown their devotion. The only exceptions are the touchy people who have just transferred from whatever neighboring church hurt them or made them mad. They will take up asylum with us until we hurt them or make them angry, then it's *sayonara.*

When Aunt Bessie or Uncle Fred or Dave from the men's Bible class appears to be hurt, the family will gather around and protect the injured one. "You have no idea what they have gone through for this church." Touchy people, like family members Bessie and Fred, have often shown more signs of love for the church than their nontouchy counterparts. How else could one explain the fact that they are still here?

If we look carefully, we see that they really do care very deeply about the church and serve it slavishly. Dave gets all in a snit about the theology taught at the Bible class because Dave cares. It matters to him. For all the ways he drives people nuts, Dave puts in long hours working on the class. He voluntarily pays attention to details. He pores over every word said or printed. He comes off as one of the most committed men in the class. He is a nuisance, but he has to be respected.

Another slant on touchy people in our churches can be put in one word: artistic. Not all touchy people are artistic, by any means. We do, however, encounter many of them who have an artistic temperament. In fact, the artistic personality has a touchiness of its own. The lone genius seeing what no one else can see can be a socially dysfunctional recluse, unable to work with other people. Almost every congregation has at least one person who has artistic gifts, an intelligence higher than the norm, a passion to do wonderful things for the church, a wonderful generosity with time—a person whose very presence shapes the personality of the whole church.

Let's face it. These people drive us batty. They do awesome things for the church, but they cannot work with any system of accountability. They may plan a grand program, but schedule it at a terrible time and in the wrong room, and do such lousy publicity that the whole thing becomes a failure. Through it all we couldn't help, because no one can make a suggestion to this person.

Artistic touchy people will gladly join any committee. Sign 'em up and wait. They will attend one meeting and quit, usually sending us a four-page, single-spaced letter explaining why they have to quit, how much it hurts, and

all the terrible things that the committee is doing. If asked to chair a committee, count on its turning into a committee of one. These dear frantic souls do
not have the gift of involving other people. They are thus inevitably frustrated
by the consequent lack of support. They are likely to jump in and do all the
work that is needed, exhausting themselves and then dashing off another four-
page, single-spaced letter, this time containing a tirade about this church not
caring and nobody helping.

These poor well-intentioned folks have great dreams for the church. But
they have zero ability to cope with the ambiguities of working with other people. They just can't handle church bureaucracy, and they become very, very
touchy.

Mercifully, artistic touchy souls do not usually have the power of nonartistic people. The family of faith tolerates them without being terrorized
by them, because the poor souls are so socially unskilled that they cannot
mount much support. The family just shrugs them off. "He's artistic, you
know."

Having rambled through various touchy types, let's see if we can make any
sense of attempts to help them thrive in the family of faith.

1. As we said in chapter 1, we are unwise to launch a search-and-destroy
mission against all touchy people. We are much better served by watching
how the family has learned to cope with them. What authority has been given
to Mr. Touchy? In what ways have people learned to work around or with Mrs.
Touchy? In almost all cases, the family will have adjusted quite adequately.
For all the difficulties these personalities cause, we need to curb our instinct
to take on our touchy parishioner. Unless there are extenuating conditions, our
best advice is this: learn to live with the situation.

2. Remember that just because a person is touchy does not mean that the
person is wrong. The four-page, single-spaced letter might have some wisdom to it. We need to listen to everyone, including touchy people.

3. In the case of the artistic touchy, our best tactic is to save them from
themselves. Where possible, keep them away from boards and committees.
They just can't hack it. Why set them up for failure? If possible, find tasks that
require creativity and can be done alone. By "done alone" I mean "done
alone." That means no coordinating with a committee, no accountability to
another person or group. Lay out all the ground rules in advance. Have clearance from all who need to give clearance, and get out of the way. These people bring tremendous gifts to the fellowship. When we can turn them loose to
run with their gifts, the whole church benefits.

4. For nonartistic touchy people the advice is just the opposite. We should
consider putting them on a board or committee. They may turn down the nom-

ination, since they might feel it is a demotion. They much prefer being free from accountability, able to criticize from the sidelines. Putting them on the ruling board, for example, might take advantage of their commitment to the church, while teaching them how decisions are made. It also defangs touchy people. They cannot so easily say, "Look what *they* are doing." Our touchy friends are now part of the "they."

5. Gradually, begin to educate the family to realize that people are responsible for their own emotions. Victor Frankl once observed that the last freedom we have is the freedom to choose our own attitude. In an odd way, this insight begins to bring the touchy person into the family. I say "in an odd way" because what I am about to say appears disrespectful of the touchy persons, although we are showing them great respect by making them accountable for their own lives.

I came into the office one day and found shell-shocked secretaries. They seemed afraid to tell me the news. I feared a fatality or some other catastrophe. So it was with some relief that I heard one secretary force out the words, "Mr. So-and-so was in here looking for you, and he is on the warpath." My guess was that in all probability So-and-so had dropped both "O" words with great gusto to anyone who would listen.

My stock answer is my method in the office of reacting to upset parishioners and to "O" words. I say, "So what?" or "That's his problem." I understand that the office staff often will have no idea what to do with my response. They had naturally assumed that when a parishioner gets upset, the parishioner has taken the role of an upset teacher or parent. We are to play the role of student or child and correct our behavior, so that the authority figure (upset person) will not punish us. The news that "So-and-so is on the warpath" is expected to make us cower before So-and-so and beg forgiveness, mend our ways, and do anything not to be sent to our rooms or spanked by So-and-so. By saying "So what?" or "That's his problem" we change the whole perception of the situation. So-and-so is an adult and therefore responsible for his or her actions and emotions. We are also adults, who hope So-and-so can get over whatever it is that seems to have caused emotional turmoil. We may even help in the process, but we are not going to hide under our desks in fear of So-and-so. The tyranny of the touchy does not go around here.

6. Sometimes the moment arrives when we have to curb a touchy person. As I have said, we are wise to err on the side of patience. The times to act, especially if the action is bold, are rare. Even when the situation does demand action, it is better to take action patiently, with understanding. Aunt Bessie, Uncle Fred, Dave, and the lady who sent Christmas cards are precious people, loved by God. They are fragile and need to be handled with care. What we

have here, ladies and gentlemen, is a unique opportunity to demonstrate Christian love in a setting where diplomacy is required.

Touchy people simmer as a perpetual source of conflict within the church. In dealing with them we need to see that our denominational ways of doing things are in full operation. That is our criterion for action. We know that it is time to act when the fellowship is not able to hold open discussion because a touchy person does not allow discussion. The topic itself is said to be too threatening to the person. Since discussion is the lifeblood of the way our congregations make decisions, we have to act. If such a touchy person is on a decision-making panel, we must go to that person ahead of time and say that we are going to be discussing an issue that we know is troubling. Perhaps the person would be more comfortable staying home or leaving the room during the debate. We hope that the person can be with us and hang in there. Regardless of whether the person decides to be in the room or absent, the discussion must be held.

Unless we are convinced that God wants us to spend our discussion time figuring out how we can smooth the ruffled feathers of a person who has once again fallen into a snit, our task is to keep the group on its intended focus. If it is the mission committee, we need to focus on mission. If it is the Christian education committee, we need to focus on Christian education.

Finally, decisions are made by the ruling board. At the end of the meeting, if the debate has been turbulent, we try to make sure everyone can at least live with the decision. We should always lay down a rule long before we have any hot debates that no one is permitted to second-guess a decision out in the parking lot after the meeting. If a person has a problem with what the ruling board is doing, speak now or forever hold your peace. To sit through a discussion, be present for the vote, go through the postdecision discussion of being able to live with it, and then go out and try to undermine the decision is a cowardly act. The ruling board will agree to this policy and will get a kick out of our threat to humiliate, at the next meeting, anyone we catch second-guessing out in the parking lot.

When it is found in the meeting that someone cannot live with a decision just made, then we need to spend whatever time is required wrestling with how we will agree to disagree. If someone feels he or she must leave the church over a decision, so be it. We will try to do everything we can to keep the fellowship together, affirm our diversity, and treat each other with respect as adults. We have to go on, trying to follow our Lord.

Will these steps bring tranquillity to our congregation? Of course not. Whoever said a family was supposed to be tranquil?

Chapter 15

It's Not about Us

*W*hat makes conflict so painful for us clergy types is that we take it personally. At times we have good reason, as when we receive a note that reads something like this: "You are a terrible minister. You are a disgrace to Christianity. You are a worthless no good bum and I hope you die." I have received nonsubtle letters just like that. When they are based on one of my failures, the letters hit like a ton of bricks. Those are letters I should take personally, very personally. They should be a wake-up call for me to do better.

This chapter will take us in a different direction. Most of the angry mail I receive is not about me or my ministry at all. Let's begin with that same angry letter and take it to its more likely conclusion. "You are a terrible minister. You are a disgrace to Christianity. You are a worthless no good bum and I hope you die. How could you possibly have decided to have us sing only two of the four stanzas of the final hymn? Have you no sense at all?" OK. It was not a major pastoral failure. In fact, we don't think it was a failure at all. Nonetheless, such a letter, however trite the conclusion, can ruin our day. How do we just brush that kind of epistle aside and move on as if nothing happened?

To trace it further, our dreaded next encounter with the letter writer may very well be shockingly cordial. The person seems to have no qualms about seeing us. He or she starts up a pleasant chitchat with us as if nothing has happened. We begin to wonder if someone else wrote the letter and affixed this person's name, as a prank. When we bring up the letter, in part to see if this is indeed the author, we find the person quite cheery about the whole incident. Then it is as if a light goes on in the letter writer's mind. "Oh, I do hope you didn't take any of what I said personally. I was just blowing off steam. I do hear people complaining about not singing all the stanzas." At the end of the conversation we are left dizzy, in total confusion. We wonder, What was that all about?

What it is all about is that people have no idea how emotionally vulnerable pastors are. We may try to steel our feelings, but we cannot. There is too much of who we are wrapped up in what we do. We figure any criticism or second-guessing is obviously aimed at us. So OK. Let's admit it. We too can be touchy. Maybe that's why touchy people bug us so much. They remind us of ourselves. That is not, however, where we are going in this chapter.

In an age of overstatement and hyperbole, when folks are in the habit of dehumanizing public figures, hurling all kinds of barbs just to get a hearing, letter writers and clergy critics figure they can unload both barrels on us without causing any harm or doing anything naughty. To make matters worse, some folks figure we are emotionless critters who are so professional, so up there in the pulpit above everybody, that we don't hurt the way mortals do. Parishioners are dumbfounded at the thought they might have wounded us.

One woman came to me once to confide that she hoped her husband's harshness did not offend me. I should not take it personally, she said. "That's just his way." I wished she had told me sooner. I also wished I could take her advice and not be offended or in any way bothered. I could not.

Another man explained to me that he would fight like a pit bull for his position until the decision was officially made. Then he would go along with the decision, giving it his full support. I found this to be a very helpful and comforting insight into his nature. It did not, however, ease the ache of the tooth marks in my psyche from his previous attacks.

Abrupt, abrasive people want to play a role in the church. They want to have their say in no uncertain terms. They don't want us to take it personally. While I have yet to learn how to anesthetize myself to the pain from some critics' unique ability to get under my skin, I have at least come to peace with knowing that a high percentage of it all is not meant personally, though I still take it that way. People are venting. Intensity and anguish have welled up for various reasons within them. They have developed an uncanny and discomforting knack for uncorking their rage around church, and that means around me.

A very helpful lesson was learned more than two decades ago in a difficult pastoral situation. A woman I cared about very much was dying of cancer. She and her husband had been leaders in the church for many, many years. They had acted as grandparents to our children, hosting our family often at meals. She was one of the most pleasant persons I had ever met. Now I stood at her bedside seeing her for one of the last times. As I held her hand she asked me to go get Doctor So-and-so to come to her room immediately. She wanted him to do something I knew he could not do. The exact request does not matter. What matters is that I hemmed and hawed and tried to talk around it. Suddenly, it was as if an evil force took hold of her. A nature I had never seen in her caused her to squeeze my hand, glare at me, and literally spit out an order that I had better get that doctor and get him pronto if I knew what was good for me.

Needless to say, I was taken aback by her hostility. But I could handle it because I knew it was not the woman I had known for years who was talking. It was the cancer talking. This is an insight we share with families who have just been worked over by a terminally ill loved one.

It is an insight that has helped ease some of the pain from conflict and criticism. Very often it is not the person talking. It is pain talking through the person. Yes, sometimes pain or a painful situation can unleash feelings that have been pent up for some time. Yes, a real part of the person is coming out, but I have taken what comfort I can from knowing that in many instances *that person* is not attacking *this person*. Instead it is some other factor just being vented into the atmosphere.

We see it in grief situations. We notice inordinate criticism aimed at the people who break the news that a relative has died. "She came out to the waiting room trying to look sympathetic, but she didn't care. You could tell by the arrogant way she tilted her head. She said it so matter-of-factly: 'I'm afraid he has died.' What a terrible way to say it. I have a good mind to report her to the higher-ups in the hospital." The anger that death stole a loved one has been transferred to the person who broke the news. It happens.

Anger at God for letting a loved one die is often transferred to us and to our church. On occasion, we encounter people who go ballistic over some minor detail in planning the funeral. Most of us are professional enough to understand what is happening and to carry on.

Less easy to understand are the emotionally charged conflicts over what should be standard operating procedures. A proposal that the church consider a new curriculum is met with hostile overreaction from a man on the ruling board. What we may not know is that the man had a shouting match with his daughter just before leaving home for the meeting. What we should remember is that his wife was the one who recommended the curriculum we are now using. Recently her health has not been good. He not only still has his fighting gloves on from the brawl with his daughter. He is also trying to protect his wife from what he rightly perceives as an act that will personally hurt her at exactly the time she can't take another hurt. He may say some rough things. He may be perceived as overreacting. He may look irrational. He may turn some of his rage on us. It helps to know that some of the debate over the curriculum is really not about the curriculum, and the barbs at us are really not about us.

Churches, remember, are families. When the family gathers, everyone brings to the moment a myriad of experiences and a pack of emotions. Family is the place where we can let our guard down a bit. Family is where a question like "How was school?" can trigger an outburst. Family is supposed to be a safe environment for venting the insecurities, uncertainties, anxieties, and angers that are eating away at us. At its best, family is a place where we can get feelings off our chests while respecting each other. At home, we put up with an extra amount of emotional outburst from each other because we are bound in covenant to each other. We know we are in this with each other for the long haul.

Our task (get this) is to try to hold together a family that isn't a family, as if it were a family, while permitting the venting that is so helpful in a family setting, without causing so many hurt feelings that scores of people leave the church. I don't think they pay us enough to do this!

Instinctively people feel they can express their feelings a bit more honestly at us in the ministry than they can at other people. They feel they can do this because of our assumed spiritual toughness, which enables us to take it. To any laypersons reading this paragraph: Your pastor is more vulnerable than you think. To pastors reading this paragraph: Our role is to let people vent as long as they do it in appropriate ways.

I recall a staff meeting where we were noting the tremendous amount of complaining and bickering we were hearing from so many people. After lengthy open discussion, we found that the negativity was really not voiced in the influential centers of the congregation. Nor was there any one program or person catching the brunt of it. We just heard generalized complaining around the drinking fountain. Then we decided to name names and name complaints. Doing so was an eye-opener. The only common thread we could discern was that the complaining people were all getting along in years. Other than church, which was making a concerted effort to draw on their abilities, they did not have any outlets in their lives to make them feel worthwhile. Their bodies and their faculties were slipping. They were mad at life, and they needed a place to vent their frustration. With tongue only slightly in cheek, we decided that it was our role as pastors of their church to give them things to complain about so they could let off steam. As a staff, we decided we were obviously serving them well because we were getting lots of negativity out of them.

The theme of this section is that a lot of "stuff" gets brought to church and dumped there. By "stuff," I refer to more than the debris left at church for the annual sale or the thrift shop. I refer to the emotions that get dumped in the church by people who find in the fellowship a place where they can let off a little steam. The point of all this is to say that a lot of the negativity swirling around, even that with our name on it, hurtful as it is, is probably not really about us.

I recall a session meeting where we were having at it. The issue was reasonably important, and the discussion was heated. As one speaker after another put his or her two cents into the discussion, a clear conflict was developing, with people drawing to one side or the other. As the heat was rising, I did a pastoral inventory of elders seated around the table. To my left was a man who was scheduled for exploratory surgery later that week. He was quite scared, but did not want anyone but me to know. Next to him sat a woman who had just had to let go some people at work, and it was tearing her up. Next to her was another woman, whose son had just been accused of drug possession at college. The school was investigating whether to throw him out. Around the table: a man whose wife had recently asked him for a separation; a woman who had not been nominated president of a garden club, as she had hoped to be; a man who had been downsized; a surgeon being sued; a person bored with life, wondering why to carry on, obviously a few cocktails into his evening. The rulers of the church are a collection of wounded people, so wounded I marveled that they were dedicated enough to show up at all. Little wonder they were lighting into each other. They were hurting personally, and this was the place to which they could come not only to seek God's will for the church, but also to act out a needed therapy for their lives. Lots of feelings had been welling up in these people. Now, on this agenda issue, they spilled out. So I was reawakened to the helpful insight that anything nasty they might say about me in this setting was probably not about me at all. Such is life in the church.

Permit me, before closing this section, to add one more angle. The reader may find this to be so outrageous as to undermine the credibility of everything written in these pages. All I ask is that you hear it out. My experience tells me that in certain kinds of churches, over the past few generations, this thought is right on.

My hunch is that the congregations I have served have done more than their part to elect Republicans to office. In fact, it was my feeling during the 1980s that were I to have questioned the teaching of Jesus, there would have been raised eyebrows. Had I questioned the teaching of Ronald Reagan, there would have been swords drawn. My father endorsed Richard Nixon in 1960, and was universally hailed as a courageous voice of truth. In 1964 he endorsed Lyndon Johnson, and people left the same church in droves for his meddling in politics. I still run into people upset about his '64 sermons.

Now you would think that a Republican congregation would be most happy when a Republican was in the White House. One might suppose that when these people get their way in an election, they would think all is well in the kingdom.

Not so fast. Deep down, people agree with John Calvin that all is not well in the kingdom. Our lives have not worked out as we had hoped. Our health has had more than a few scares. Our job is not as fulfilling as we thought it would be. Our marriage has its ups and downs, and lately a lot of flat times. All around us people seem to have less integrity, less civility, less old-fashioned decency. People are worried that we are not secure in this country and the future is uncertain. In short, something is wrong with our lives.

People cannot figure out exactly what it is that has put the unrest in their souls. Sadly, even church people have not connected the dots to see that the picture painted in Scripture describes it to a tee. Human sinfulness plagues our lives. We are collectively and individually a major cause of our own malaise.

Instead of working through the doctrine of sin, church folks try to figure who to blame for their sense that all is not well. When a Democrat is in the White House the answer is obvious: "It's that fool president." The year 2000, as I began to write these pages, found my life incredibly happy, not simply because I had returned to my home church but also because the Democrat Bill Clinton was a marvelous scapegoat. Rational or not, justified or not, President Clinton bore the sins of us all.

In my last parish we had an ugly hassle over a property issue. The ill will did not clear up for a while, in part because the Republican George Bush the First was president. When life was not what it ought to be, good Republican Presbyterians could not blame the president. "It's that fool preacher." With the election of Bill Clinton, there was a gloom on the faces of parishioners who were sure we were on the road to ruin. Now I'll let you in on a little secret: almost all my problems of the immediate past evaporated. Church attendance went back up. I could do no wrong. Every day another parishioner put yet another anti-Clinton cartoon on my desk. All the concerns about my leadership where now on his shoulders. I was back in the good graces of all.

As a sidebar to my theory, I add this: The absolute worst time for a pastor of a Republican congregation is not only when a Republican is in office, but when that Republican is twisting in the wind. All the dreads and angst in the souls of saints come to a boil. "Something is really wrong now. That fool preacher has got to be purged from our midst as an offering to appease whatever demons are attacking our beloved president."

It all sounds outrageous. My father's ministry collapsed in conflict during Watergate. During the Iran-Contra affair, I watched a neighboring congregation mount a vicious campaign against its pastor. Oddly, when President Reagan escaped unharmed from Iran-contra, the hostile campaign evaporated into thin air.

Maybe it's all just a crazy notion. For what little truth you may ascribe to this thesis, it is one more example of how people in church get into conflicts, complain and vent their rage at us, when it really is quite often not about us at all. It's just that they need a safe place to let it all out.

Chapter 16

Coping

Anyone who dares to write about how to cope with conflict and crisis in the parish needs to begin by admitting how terribly difficult such coping is. Though most donnybrooks in the parish are not about us, we feel that in some way all of them are, and to be sure more than a few are. In fact if we trace the implications of almost any conflict far enough, we will find ourselves somehow implicated, however remotely.

Few people can appreciate the sheer terror in the heart of a pastor when the going gets tough. There just aren't any handles we can grab onto, and our authority is tentative at best. I have chatted recently with several very able ministers who are convinced they cannot count on their congregations to support them in the crunch. They don't know if there is anywhere to turn for support. They fear that their denomination might decide they should be removed from their job. As a consequence many a pastor tries to keep the lid on the crisis for as long as possible. Sharing our anguish with colleagues is felt to be dangerous. We fear that our presumed friends will spread abroad our tale of woe, or hold it against us if another church should be looking at us as a possible candidate. An offhand comment over coffee that First Church Wherever is looking at us might be met with a solemn warning from our colleague that "I hear there is conflict in the present situation, so First Wherever ought to be careful."

Such feelings are a sad commentary on the lack of trust that permeates today's church. It is also an explanation for why conflicts get out of control before we seek help. It exemplifies how, in our panic, we catastrophize a situation, imagining that a stern-faced group of church leaders is about to come into our office and tell us it is time to move on. We are traumatized. We can point to friends in ministry who have had "the visit." Many among us have had various individuals on their own or in clusters confront us with our ineptitude, expressing the wish that we would just pack up and leave. The notion of "clergy killers" takes its root in hard fact.

On top of that, we live with the haunting awareness that even if we handle this crisis by the book, with impeccable professionalism, our ministry might be ruined anyway. These are, after all, a cluster of Smythes, this congregation we serve. We are not Smythes, of course. They have a sovereign right to dislike us, undermine us, try to run us out of town—a right far too many of them feel free to exercise.

Any effort to offer advice on how to cope with conflict must take seriously our near paralysis in the midst of being weighed down by the crisis. Such an effort at advice must humbly acknowledge how difficult it is to muster the energy and concentration to focus on doing anything. It must take seriously the hard fact that church life is ultimately out of our control. No matter how well we do, we can still be rejected and renounced. Of course, there is also the corollary: no matter how poorly we do, some forgiving souls will take us in and give us full support. In the last analysis, ministry makes little sense and cannot be programmed to react predictably.

Ministry obviously takes its toll. Health providers for clergy are aware that what seems an inordinate amount of payouts are going to therapists treating pastors and their families for depression, stress, and related emotional difficulties. Clergy marriages are at risk. Heavy use of alcohol, prescription drugs, and even occasionally illegal drugs is not uncommon. The number of highly capable pastors who leave ministry is a sign that this is not a profession that is invitingly warm and fuzzy. The low numbers of young people opting for a career in ministry is indicative that this is not considered a worthwhile calling. Ministers feel they have been beaten up long enough, and they are getting out while the getting is good. The day-to-day hassles wear pastors down, and the conflicts prove to be the refrigerator that breaks the camel's back.

Having said that, it is helpful anyway to focus on a list of basic practices that should be followed in conflict. While there is absolutely no guarantee that our ministry will survive or that folks will let up on us, there is at least the comfort of knowing that we are being faithful. When our heads are swimming in panic, we can at least know what steps to take; or at least we can rest in the confidence that we are not alone, because one other pastor has done those things and actually had them published. Making no promises that the hit team won't come to tell us to leave, making no guarantees that anything will ever work out for us, I offer a list of eight ways to cope under pressure.

1. *Preach well.* This obviously is especially good advice if the rap against us is that our preaching stinks. It is also good advice regardless of the rap.

The great pulpiteer Phillips Brooks said that preaching is the bringing of truth through personality. In the sermon segment of worship the congregation gets to see our personality perhaps more than anywhere else. In good times and bad, parishioners want to know what kind of person we are. Are we able to let the love of God flow through us, or are we all caught up in ourselves? Are we fair and objective, or do we grind an ax on our favorite issues? Are we mature or childish? Are we insightful, or are we shallow? Are we the kind of person the congregation wants and needs in the pulpit week after week, or would they not mind if they never heard from us again?

Like it or not, many people will make their decisions how to respond to whatever is the crisis du jour on the basis of how they feel about our preaching during the crisis. They want to find spiritual guidance. They need to hear what the Lord is saying to them in those moments. They want to know that for all the turmoil in this church, the congregation is at least God's family, rooted in the Lord. If the pulpit fails to provide the spiritual nourishment in this time, we have let the congregation down and deserve their indictment.

So, work on the sermons. A good idea would be to draw texts from the lectionary as a way of disciplining ourselves not to take unfair advantage of the air time the sermon affords, and so as not to be guilty of the accusation that we chose our text because we wanted to preach our own opinions or to advance our own cause. Even if we already use the lectionary, this is a good time to remind the congregation that we do: "Our lectionary text for today is . . ."

Humor helps. We don't want to use gimmicky jokes to get laughs. We certainly don't want to use anything that might even remotely be construed as putting others down (a good rule all the time). Humor can be healing if it is a form of insight or is a joke on us. It calms people. It is quite literally comic relief in a time of tension. When we are able to inject some helpful humor into our sermon, the congregation can rest in the fact that we are OK, we are leading, we are human, and our personality and message are engaging even now.

If nothing else, hard, prayerful work on a sermon deepens our walk with the Lord. Rather than stewing over our political well-being, we are reading Scripture. We read devotional material and commentaries. Our minds are creatively occupied in uplifting ways. We think compassionately about the congregation to whom this word will be delivered. Crises are moments to take time and go deeply into issues raised by the text. Wrestle with the issues raised. Sweat. Take the congregation to a place of profound revelation in the sermon. Use the crisis as a time to deepen preaching for future years. When we help people hear the voice of God speaking to their lives, they don't forget it, and they are grateful.

2. *Be their pastor.* Never let a crisis get us so distracted that hospital visits are missed, shut-ins are ignored, or people have to face the dark moments without our support. If anything, use the crisis as a reminder to ratchet up our shepherding of the flock several notches.

If there are weddings and funerals to be conducted during the conflict time, give them extra attention. These are unforgettable events in the life of any family. When the pastor sloughs off such a service, resentment builds that is not soon calmed. Weddings and funerals are a unique opportunity to introduce the church, our ministry, and our Lord to the larger community. No harm is done by giving the assembled guests the notion that this is a church with a ministry where spiritually helpful things happen.

Never do what I have seen too many fellow pastors do in a crisis—use pastoral visiting as a chance to pour out their hearts to a parishioner, while trying to curry that person's support. Pastoral care must be nonmanipulative. We don't bring up the crisis in these conversations. If the person we are visiting brings it up, we respond as objectively and with as much statesmanship as we can muster, always offering the reminder, "I am not here to talk about that." Many a pastor has testified that when her or his hour of testing came, the congregation was supportive because they had been faithfully pastored. "I may not agree with what the preacher is trying to do, but that pastor was at my mother's bedside, and I'll never forget it."

3. *Conflicts are uniquely teachable moments.* People are paying attention. Church becomes the topic of conversation in the workplace or at dinner parties. People show up at meetings they might otherwise skip. When a vote is taken, the results show an inordinately high percentage of participation. The stained-glass veneer of church lingo is shattered. People say what they really feel, and it is not always a very pretty picture. Turning conflict into an adult education opportunity can breathe new life into us. What an emotional relief it is to sense that a weighty problem is becoming an opportunity!

Without being manipulative, we can legitimately explain how our heartfelt position in this debate reflects our faith in Jesus Christ. Without trying to score points for our side in the argument, we can in fairness ask what theology is being revealed in the discussion. "What would Jesus do and why?" is a legitimate point for conversation. What kind of witness will we have if we go this way or that on the issue? What kind of church are we fighting to become? Would the Lord be glorified in such a church? What does Scripture say? Agonizing over these questions gives us a marvelous chance to grow in the faith through the case-study method. If we do not somehow see the conflict as an opportunity to learn, we will have missed a special moment and failed our parish.

4. *Crises are opportunities to demonstrate in nonmanipulative ways how one's denominational procedures are to be used.* The reader will note that the caution to be nonmanipulative is being stated repeatedly. One hopes that we are bright enough to keep our eyes open in proceeding through this minefield.

"Nonmanipulative" does not imply that we should be stupid. What it means is that preaching, pastoring, teaching, and administering are of such importance to our calling that we will not use them as means to our own personal advantage. If the congregation becomes convinced that we use the pulpit or that we pastor, teach, and administer as a means to gain advantage for ourselves, we are cooked, and ought to be.

In crisis or conflict it is mandatory that the congregation believe rightly that we serve the Lord by trusting the procedures and processes of our denomination. Where boards have the right and responsibility to decide, let them. Inform them of their power and let them hear all sides in a fair, open manner on a level playing field.

A primary advantage to playing it by the denominational rules is that we avoid a peripheral theater of hostilities. People cannot legitimately fight over the process to be followed in the debate, because the process is already spelled out clearly. As members of a denominational church we are beholden to that denomination. Folks cannot say we cooked up a process that is biased toward one side or the other.

5. *Most votes are ultimately not all that important in the long run.* Without my wanting to sound uncaring, life does go on. The Lord is still Lord. God's purpose is still being worked out. Let's never underestimate how the God who used crucifixion to bring about new life can use even our church's most unfaithful decisions to bring about justice. Who knows? The "wrongheaded decision" may have been just what the church needed to give the issue a fresh look and a new beginning.

Get this: We ourselves might be shocked to realize that the so-called pathetically "unfaithful decision" might have been the Lord's wisdom at work in the church after all. Perhaps time will show us that the venture on which we were banking our ministry was a fraud after all. It would have been a disaster had the church adopted it.

A few years ago I told my wife one Saturday night that if the congregation did not vote a certain way the next day at a congregational meeting, I intended to resign on the spot. What frightens me even now is that I might well have done it, and it would have been the dumbest, least faithful thing I could possibly have done. Mercifully, the congregation voted overwhelming the way I hoped they would, and I did not have the chance to be stupid.

I had let myself get carried away. It was self-centered pride, mostly. I wanted to be the hero, the martyr for a worthy cause, the victim of what I imagined could be an un-Christian decision. I was tired of dealing with the opposition. I felt at the time that I did not have the moxie to cope with what I thought might have been a catastrophic setback.

In retrospect I can see that it wasn't that big a deal in the long scheme of things. The Lord's work was not helped or impeded very much one way or the other by the decision going the way I hoped. I would have resigned foolishly over a rather inconsequential matter.

6. *Now, understand that the last section is more than a pious version of the ice-ball theory.* The ice ball theory, as you may recall, says that in two billion years the earth will be an ice ball, so who cares what happens now? Some people use this theory to calm their nerves and gain a mental edge. The notion has a certain elevated apathy about it, but it is not what we are trying to convey here.

Rather we are acknowledging that God is God and we are not. God is the creator of the entire cosmos, and God will be God when the last human breath is exhaled on this planet. Our efforts are feeble attempts to do our best in our time. The end result of our labors, however, is beyond our control.

In an earlier book I suggested that we are told by Jesus to abide in him and we will bear fruit. The command is to abide. We are not told to bear fruit, nor are we told what fruit is. Somehow we are led to believe that people will be fed by our abidance. That is about all we need to know. I suggested in that book that the Lord does not want us measuring and manipulating to run up the score on some mythically quantifiable fruit-bearing scale, so the Lord keeps us in the dark. It is not for us to see, count, pile up, store away, or brag about the fruits of our labors because (a) it is God's doing, not ours, and (b) we aren't altogether sure what the desired fruit is anyway.

So in this crisis that has us all in a tizzy, we are called to be faithful—abiding in Christ—and that is about it.

This is why the analogy of the Smythe family reunion proves to be a helpful image for ministry. That family, which may just now be making life miserable for us, was called together by God, is sustained by God, and used by God in ways we cannot comprehend. We are at best an activities director with precious little authority except to remind people that God is God.

At some point in the process of weathering the crisis, we are meant to find a blessed calm. That calm comes when we realize that we are not supposed to carry the whole weight of the church on our shoulders. We are not solely responsible for immediately favorable outcomes or for discerning with 100 percent accuracy what favorable outcomes are. While we continue faithfully serving the Lord by carrying out our ministry with compassion and professionalism, we come to that precious moment, usually just after turning in at the end of a long day, when we turn it all over to God. "Lord, it's your church, your people, your timing, your kingdom, your will. I am giving it to you. I cannot be and will not try to be the whole church. I will not try to be God.

I confess that I have arrogantly had a God complex, and it has worn me out. Now I'm going back to being a mortal humanoid. Good night."

It is amazing how well we'll sleep.

7. *Take care of ourselves.* Airlines have wisdom in their preflight instructions. We are told that in the event the cabin loses pressure, an oxygen bag will drop from overhead. If we are traveling with a small child, we are instructed to put on our own mask first, then help the child. This seemed for a long time rather callous to me. Shouldn't we be other-centered, caring for the child first? Then I realized that if we pass out, we will not be able to care for the little one. The child not only needs us, but needs us to be as functional as possible. For the sake of the little one, we are required to look after our own needs first in the crisis situation.

A doctor friend of mine found his job had recently doubled, if not tripled. He had just been given a tremendously time-consuming administrative responsibility on top of his already busy and growing practice. His days were about to become impossibly long. I was surprised to discover that the first thing he did on learning of his expanded duties was to schedule even more time out of his week to engage a personal trainer to put him through a vigorous physical workout several times a week. Then I realized he was wise enough to know that he could survive the draining pressure of his work only if he got into tip-top shape.

The wisdom for us is that we dare not let ourselves get run down during the crisis. When we are frazzled, exhausted, or feel "brain dead," we say things we regret and we make decisions that are just plain dumb.

We owe it to our ministry to see crisis time as a time when it is crucial that we get exercise. Depending on our age and condition, we may walk, swim, play tennis, lift weights, or get into an aerobics class.

Take time off. Get away for a day. Take an overnight.

Watch our diet.

Get to bed on time, doing all we can to rest.

Throw ourselves into a therapeutic hobby.

Read for devotion and relaxation.

Stay in touch with our doctor, and get more frequent checkups. This is a must. We need to monitor what this stress is doing to our bodies and take appropriate steps to ward off insidious repercussions.

8. *Regardless of what our theology would have us believe, the experience of a church crisis makes us realize that we are on the front lines of spiritual warfare.* Again, I say that we must be nonmanipulative, especially on this point. The power of evil is not so transparent as to reside exclusively in our opponents. We could drive all our enemies out of the church and the evil one

would still be alive and well within our fellowship. In fact, one of the shrewdest ways evil does us in is to get us believing that we are on the side of goodness and purity while our opponents are the incarnation of evil itself. Such a belief is guaranteed to prompt the most demonic words and deeds from us.

As my father was reflecting on an especially traumatic conflict in his ministry, he said, "If I hadn't already had a firm belief in the devil, I sure would have developed one during that time." While administrators, psychology majors, sociologists, and church politicians could explain my father's and almost all other crises in terms of their own particular disciplines, I side with my father's assessment that a primary cause of the difficulty was the power of evil. Yes, Virginia, there is a devil. The devil is no friend of the church.

Believing in the evil one and believing that satanic forces are brilliantly shrewd, I have realized that evil is not worried about unfaithful, stuck-in-their-ways, dead churches. They seem remarkably tranquil. Few if any conflicts pop up there. I have also observed that when we begin to see the Holy Spirit move in a fellowship, we can note that the power of evil shows up to undermine the Lord's work. We are not far off base if we realize there is a compliment paid our ministry in this present unpleasantness. Apparently, the congregation was threatening to move in a direction the power of evil did not like. Hence we have been invaded by a malicious force stirring us up. A brouhaha has broken out in ways that really make no sense. Something ugly has been unleashed in the fellowship. It is for us to identify in a nonmanipulative way the spiritual warfare that is tearing our church and our personal life apart.

In the last analysis, a lot of church conflicts are spiritual wars, the power of evil shoving us around. Conflict is a good time to go into the privacy of our study, get down on our knees, and pray a prayer of thanksgiving to God that our church has been faithful enough to upset the evil one; to pray that the church will continue to be faithful, to call on the name of Jesus, to offer ourselves anew to the Lord's service. This is a time to draw closer to our Lord, praying that the Lord will enter the fray, not to give us a victory in the squabble, but so that the Lord will be Lord of the church.

Chapter 17

The Body of Christ

*O*ne thing I really like about the Bible is that it is so "biblical." When we are in a tight jam in our congregation and the Bible has a clear-cut, slam-dunk obvious word of wisdom for us on the subject, who can argue? No one wants to be exposed as being "unbiblical." So when Paul wrote 1 Corinthians 12 especially, I am convinced, for my ministry, he gave me and all church leaders a biblical trump card we can play when congregational life gets a tad testy.

First Corinthians 12 was written to a turned-on church. Stuff was happening. All kinds of groups were geared up, enthused, vying for space on the calendar and agenda of First Church Corinth. Since conflict is often the consequence of vitality, Corinth had all kinds of trouble. Paul had to write them explaining how to get along, how to coexist, how to appreciate sisters and brothers who go at discipleship in ways we find odd, how to feel included and needed by the rest of the congregation when we feel terribly out of place ourselves.

Paul's analogy is brilliant. He writes that the church is the body of Christ. Like all bodies, the body of Christ has many diverse parts, which perform different functions. He said in effect that we cannot hear with our foot, and we cannot walk with our ear, nor should we try. For us to be physically able people, we need our different body parts performing their diverse tasks, one hopes with a modicum of coordination. "For just as the body is one and has many members, and all the members of the body, though many, are one body, so it is with Christ. . . . Now you are the body of Christ and individually members of it" (vv. 12, 27).

Think about it. Anyone wanting to see the arms, legs, eyes, and hands of Jesus in today's world should wander into a house of worship some Sunday morning and take a peek. The body of Christ is seated in the pews. Hard as it may be for some folks to grasp, by the work of the Holy Spirit our congregation is Jesus in the flesh today. We are the body of Christ. One only hopes and prays that people recognize the Lord when they take a look at us.

Now if we take seriously this most helpful image of the church, and if we pay attention to how Paul develops his analogy for the Corinthians, we can readily spot principles for leadership, which are nothing short of a blessing. We can have a framework with which to consider some of the most basic conflicts that eat away at even the finest of congregations. Should we or should we not let these people begin that new strange-sounding program in our church? How do we minister to the people who feel marginalized because the power brokers of the congregation do not cotton to their style of discipleship? How do we relate to the cast of characters who have won the king of the ecclesiastical hill game and now won't let anyone else play? How do we hold the church together when some folks insist that anyone who does not do the faith their way is going straight to hell? How do we pastor the poor soul who believes she has to be at everything the church does, and now the church is doing too much for her to attend? How do we soothe the panicked chap who is scared that "if we let those people do that, it'll ruin the church I've loved for sixty years"?

This analogy of the body makes a marvelously helpful point. In order for any one of us to be aligned with the body of Christ, we need other people. No matter how hard I try, I cannot be that body all by myself. Christianity is not an individual sport. We need the fellowship of the church to play. Let's look at this truth in action.

1. When we have been in the preaching ministry for a time we notice something. The congregation to which we preach demonstrates a personality of its own. We sense it while we preach. Sometimes the personality is bubbly and responsive. Other times it is solemn. When we are preaching to a congregation we can sense the mood, the level of fatigue, the settledness or unsettledness, the attentiveness or easy distraction. We begin to sense that beyond the faces staring at us this congregation is a live animal listening, reacting, emoting before us. I wonder if Paul felt that. Was that the feeling that led him to say the congregation is the body of Christ?

People sense it when they visit a congregation. They talk about the church as they might talk about an individual they just met. "That is a friendly church [person]." "That church [person] is really cold." "The church [person] has a deep interest in helping the poor." "That church [person] seems to be having a tough time of it right now."

The first point Paul makes is that the congregation can be viewed as one personality.

2. The second point is that to be the body of Christ we need to be in fellowship with people who bring to the family what we do not. We need people who have gifts we do not have, a perspective from which we do not see, a role

to play that is not our role. The concept of the church's being a homogeneous unit is pure heresy, because we cannot be the body of Christ if we are all the same. Diversity is mandatory—without diversity within the congregation we simply cannot be the body of Christ.

Admittedly, I warm to Paul's call to diversity for very personal reasons. I have good friends who mean a lot to me and for whom I have tremendous respect on both sides of the great divide in today's church. The committees that drafted opposing amendments on the gay ordination issue were both chaired by friends of mine. Further, as I listen to persons on each side of the debate state their case, their faith touches my heart. These people obviously love the Lord, take Scripture seriously, and have a well-reasoned position. They are convincing. Yet, inevitably, I feel that I am not hearing from either side the whole gospel about the whole Jesus as introduced in the whole Bible. I need some of what the persons on each side bring to the table. For me, the voice of God speaks most clearly as friends and colleagues bring both sides to the discussion. Were my friends and colleagues no longer in tension with each other because they were no longer in the same church, neither of their new denominations could adequately nourish my soul. So I struggle to be an agent of reconciliation for the admittedly selfish reason that only when both sides exist together in tension is the gospel articulated in a way that feeds my soul.

In my own Presbyterian denomination I have tried to bring representatives of both sides together. I have rejoiced when each meeting has seen barriers broken down. I saw a ray of hope when one such meeting called the church to a sabbatical. Rather than keep trotting the same people to the microphones to offer the same arguments on the same issue, I had hoped we would let matters cool so that new levels of dialogue could occur. I had hoped the two sides would spend more time talking to each other instead of plotting to do each other in. I had hoped we would show ourselves to be the body of Christ.

I am among those who feel that most mainline denominations have a healthy diversity, but an unhealthy way of acting it out. We begin to feel like children of a troubled marriage. We love both our parents and both sides of our family, but an icy chill, a simmering resentment, a profound lack of trust, and more than an occasional loud outburst signal trouble. What scares many of us most is that if there were to be a divorce, we would want to spend time with both separated partners and could not see ourselves exclusively with one, without the other. In today's church many of us are at risk of becoming the lost children of an angry divorce.

Paul's plea is that we coexist in a dynamically diverse fellowship called the body of Christ. His plea is timely for the denominational church. It is challenging wisdom for our congregations.

3. We need to be sensitive to the inevitable hurt that certain people will feel as a family of faith grows. We can see how it happens. Lots of groups begin to meet. New ministries spring up. The church calendar looks quite busy as these different activities keep the building lit up more nights of the week. Folks who love the church and want to give it their total support suddenly come up against a real problem. "There's more going on here than I can possibly attend." Understand that only people who love the church say that. They have always believed that when the church family has a meeting they have a responsibility to be there. This is, after all, their family. Now the sheer busyness of the church's activity wears them out. They begin to miss some gatherings, which gives them a very deflating sense that they are being estranged from the family they have always known. "My family is meeting without me." Such a feeling is never comfortable.

Add to that feeling the sense that "some of this new stuff going on around here doesn't feel right. It is not my cup of tea." This devoted soul may have just attended a meeting to set up a brand-new kind of ministry. The poor person realizes he or she has no abilities in this area of service and cannot even understand what the folks are talking about. Nothing of the meeting resonates with any aspect of this person's church experience. The poor soul feels like a fish out of water in his or her own church.

Helping this member of the church family understand that he or she does not have to attend all those meetings will have a number of effects. It will be at once hurtful for the person, as well as profoundly instructive and in the end quite liberating, though it may not at first feel that way. Perhaps for the first time a pillar of the church is learning that there are some facets of our church's work that are "not for me." Some things will have to happen in the church without this person's knowing about it or having input on it. A part of the church will get along quite nicely without this person. It all feels "out of control." That can't help but elicit an emotional tug.

Our job is to help people understand that this is as it should be. The body of Christ image helps us explain the value of having more going on than any of us can experience. In fact, the best way to model this is for us to let people see that we ourselves cannot attend everything. Nor should we. We do not have to be on top of everything. The Holy Spirit can move quite well in a room with the pastor absent. Some say the Spirit moves better in the pastor's absence, but let's not go there just now.

The point is that the brilliant image Paul has developed about the congregation being the body of Christ allows us to help devoted saints of the parish realize they are only a part of the body. For us to be a congregation akin to what we find in the New Testament, this church needs to be so diverse that no one of us, including the pastor, can possibly participate fully in all of it. We all need to trust the Lord and let go for the church to blossom.

4. The corollary to people realizing that they do not have to participate in everything is the inclusive word to that other person who wonders, Do I belong at all? Does my particular giftedness have a place in this family?

When people become a part of a particular ministry in the church, especially if it is a newly formed ministry, it takes very little to make them and their ministry feel unwanted. Perhaps it is a group for young singles. The night they hoped to use the church parlor, the room was already booked. The secretary forgot to type a line in their bulletin announcement. The minister was out of town and did not return the leader's phone call for thirty-six hours. The custodian put out coffee, but forgot the hot water and tea bags, and they had specifically asked for tea bags, I want you to know! The room they had to meet in was too hot. They can take a hint. "That church does not really want us."

Realizing that many people are brittle and feel quite tentative about their involvement, we need a strong dose of 1 Corinthians 12. The best strategy for putting 1 Corinthians 12 at a cornerstone of our ministry is to develop an instinct to say, "Yes." Our motto must be "Go for it."

We've been over this before, but I cannot emphasize it enough. We hear the suggestion: "A group of us have been praying together, and we feel led to start a tutoring program in an inner-city neighborhood." We should respond, "Yes. Go for it."

Folks come to our study to ask, "Could some of us have a room Wednesday nights to pray, sing, and study Scripture? Judy has had an experience called 'baptism in the Holy Spirit.' She does what is called 'speaking in tongues.' Can we make that a part of what we do on Wednesdays?" We say, "Yes. Go for it."

A voice on the phone says, "Some guys want to get together for breakfast one morning a week; just guys talking about guy issues, sharing prayer concerns, and maybe having a speaker. Is that OK?" We answer, "Yes. Go for it."

Someone stops us at the coffee hour. "I want to start a parents' group." We say, "Yes. Go for it."

A teenager says, "We don't get turned on by the hymns in church. Can we start a music group that would occasionally lead singing Sunday morning?" We say, "Yes. Go for it."

We get a letter. "We'd like to develop a partnership with a nearby congregation different racially from ours. Maybe we could exchange pulpits and choirs sometimes. Maybe the youth groups could do stuff together. Maybe we could have a picnic with them sometime." We write back, "Yes. Go for it."

It is vital that we be a loud, consistent voice saying yes. We all know there will be plenty of loud voices saying no. Other members of the church might not see the need for this new ministry. Some folks might feel it is dangerous. Colleagues will question our sanity. Some folks will feel it is contrary to their understanding of the church. Yes, many of these requests will have to be put through our ever-blessed committee structure. Of course the old standbys will inevitably get trotted out: "We've never done it that way before!" "We tried that a few years ago and it didn't work." "I know a church that tried that, and it split the church."

We need to remind ourselves and our parish that Paul wrote, "The eye cannot say to the hand, 'I have no need of you.'" (v. 21a). "Indeed, the body does not consist of one member but of many" (v. 14). Over the course of my ministry I have, I hope, made it a high priority to hold back the naysayers who try to stifle new ministries. Regrettably, I have not been perfect, often being a blocker myself. It has at least been my intent, in my own fallen way, to follow 1 Corinthians 12 and let diversity happen, let a variety of gifts be expressed, and let as much of the body be present as possible.

The notion first dawned on me as style for ministry in the 1960s, when churches were of a divided mind whether to get involved in social action or whether to do evangelism. My perception was that most churches did neither very well, but they surely squabbled about it.

In those years 1 Corinthians 12 spoke to me with real freshness. I wondered how the church of Jesus Christ could say to workers for justice, "You have no place in the fellowship." If these people were led to social action, I wanted them to know they had my full support and I would work with them. A similar small cadre of persons wanted to do evangelism and open the door to spiritual renewal. How could anyone justifiably oppose that? So I gave them full support. In times like that I have always wanted to write Paul a thank-you note for that twelfth chapter of First Corinthians. His teaching of the body and diversity of gifts is fundamental to healthy congregations.

I soon noticed then what was happening. When the church started a ministry to the poor, a number of people in the congregation felt estranged. Certain people could not see themselves getting involved with the poor. They were very uncomfortable with "their" church validating a form of discipleship that was outside their own personal frame of reference. They feared that they would be indicted for not participating. "If the church sends people to help in a soup kitchen but I cannot go along, their doing what I do not feel called to do makes me feel that I am being judged. So I will oppose them. I don't want them doing that in my church." These folks were just plain scared. Quite a bit was at stake for them. They were not just opposing social action or evangelism. They were fighting, however irrationally, to hold on to their legitimate place in the family.

By turning to 1 Corinthians 12, I could point out to them what it means to be "biblical" in the local congregation. There is a variety of gifts. There are different parts of the body. That group is gifted in social ministry. That is their thing. Many among us are not inclined to do that. Some in the church have gifted vocal cords. They sing in the choir. That does not mean everyone has to have a good singing voice or sing in the choir. It means we need one another to be the body of Christ. Let's let the people with a gift and call to social ministry do it, and thank God for them. Let's let the ones gifted and called to evangelism do it, and thank God for them. Let's let the singers sing and the teachers teach and the administrators administrate and the deacons deke and the preachers preach. Celebrating the fact that a few among us have a particular calling does not in any way judge or even question those of us (phrases like "those of us" are important to let persons feel we identify with them) who do not have that calling. The task of the pastor is to help the naysayer feel included and wanted too, while we energetically support a new ministry that is not the naysayer's cup of tea.

5. Having gone to the mats to help a ministry get started and be a part of the church's life, we now have to discipline the very ministry we have just affirmed. Our word to a newly started group is clearly stated again and again. "I am delighted that the Lord has gifted you with a ministry like this. I will help you be a vital part of this church. I'll help get you meeting rooms, funds, publicity. I'll be with you. I will defend you before any of your critics. You are a very important part of this church family, but you are not the whole family. I do not want to hear you putting down someone who has not joined you in your activity. I do not want to hear you saying someone is less than Christian because she or he is not joining you in your group. Do not complain if you have to share bulletin board space, or if I cannot be at all your gatherings, or if your announcement gets cut. You are a vital part of our family, but you are not the whole family. There is more to this church than your program. I will fight to see that you are included in the fellowship, but I will fight just as hard to see that you do not take over this fellowship."

"If the whole body were an eye, where would the hearing be? If the whole body were hearing, where would the sense of smell be?" (v. 17) I am convinced that if all church folk made it a habit of reading 1 Corinthians 12 and living by the injunctions laid out in that marvelous chapter, church life would not only go better, it would come alive.

Part V

Commitment to Stewardship and Mission

Chapter 18

Commitment

When we showed up to become pastor of a five-hundred-member church, we might have been naive enough to assume that we would encounter five-hundred Spirit-filled disciples of the risen Christ wholly committed to doing the Lord's work. We might have had the mistaken impression that our task would be to equip and then coordinate the dynamic ministries of the five-hundred. Not so. In fact, we may never in this lifetime set eyes on the five-hundred, and we will certainly never see them all together in one place at the same time under any circumstance whatsoever. Forty-five of them will in all probability have left town by the time we get there. Two of them will have joined another church but never informed our church of their departure. Three more, having moved out of state, will have died and of course would be unable to let us know of their demise, and their survivors did not think to let us in on it either. Of those resident living souls, the majority take a "We'll call you if we need you" attitude toward all matters ecclesiastical.

What a crushing disillusionment it is to discover that when a church declares that it has five-hundred active members, that congregation is not telling the truth. To be sure, they can produce a list with five-hundred names written on it, but there is no way they can produce five-hundred disciples of Jesus Christ to go with those names. Our first shock is in realizing that the church is actually a great deal smaller in membership than we had supposed.

It should not have taken us long to figure out this is not a church of five-hundred "active" members, unless we are in complete denial. The tour of the church building back during our interview with the search committee should have been a clue for us. Our tour guide might have been jabbering on about five-hundred faithful people serving the Lord in this place. When we came to the sanctuary, which seats 225, we were told, with a proud smile, that this room is "very ample for our one service of worship. In fact, you'll be able to build attendance in a room as big as this." Even if we were only partially awake, we could immediately figure there is one thing we know for sure about these five-hundred wonderful people: the overwhelming majority of them do not regularly worship Almighty God on Sunday in this sanctuary.

Yet we seem unwilling to face the reality, especially after we have arrived. Our pride, particularly as we converse with our colleagues in ministry, will cause us to latch on to illusions and to live with our own special form of denial. Learning that the average Sunday attendance from September to May is 170, we announce to our peers that we are serving a church where a full third of the membership attends worship every Sunday. We win points with the club, since in our denial world one-third of membership actually attending worship is considered at least par for the course. The general consensus that we try to create among our colleagues is that we must be pretty good with the sermon to get a third of our membership to show up every week. Never mind that when we factor in the summer numbers, the average attendance drops to 159.

A few problems emerge, however, as we fine-tune who makes up the 170 average attenders. On a typical Sunday, Jane gets Fred to come with her. Fred is not a member, nor are the three little ones who tag along with them. In fact, as we look around the sanctuary we discover twenty to twenty-five children who are still too young to be counted as members. Marge and Sam will never join, but they are in attendance every week from September to June. Five kids from the local college are there on average, and five other nonmember visitors show up on any given Sunday.

So let's face reality. There are not one-third of the membership present on Sunday morning. The hard facts reveal that the church's commitment is far, far worse than we try to claim.

Then as we listen to why the five-hundred wonderful people cannot come to church or bring the kids to Sunday school, even more illusions will drop away. Of the many excuses given, some are quite legitimate. "We have the flu." "We travel to take care of my mother." "We are away four months of the year." But, alas, most of the excuses are smoke screens. "I decided to work in the yard." "We were not in the mood." "We have a brunch that we have to attend." Then we have the real bugaboo. "Megan has a soccer game." (I've not done a thorough investigation, and so my data do not have any scholarly credibility. It seems to me that 94.6 percent of all little girls named Megan never miss any soccer event for any Sunday school event in any church anywhere.) Once in a sermon I challenged our community's idolatrous loyalty to kiddy soccer that takes children away from church events. It was not one of my more popular homiletical efforts.

Actually, we cannot expect our children to live by a higher standard than the adults. Truth be told, the local country clubs regularly hold Sunday morning outings and tournaments. On those occasions there is no question that our country-clubbers will be on the links and not in the pews. In fact, most of them don't need a tournament or even a nice day to stay away from church to play a round of golf. Open the club and the church might as well shut down, as far as these persons are concerned.

Let's face reality. Many persons who have publicly said that Jesus Christ is their Lord and Savior have a deeper commitment to golf or to soccer than they do to worshiping God or learning about Jesus.

If the worship statistics are not disillusioning enough, stewardship will soon come along and really do us in. Even though some among us dread asking for money, almost all of us sense the excitement that sweeps through a congregation as the stewardship committee begins its work. A theme is picked. A vision is talked about for the coming year. Speakers present "Minutes for Stewardship" during worship. Posters are put up on the walls, showing what can happen if everybody steps up by X amount per week. The church begins to feel the possibilities of what will happen when the pledge cards come in and we go over the top. Five-hundred committed Christians working together can do wonderful things for the Lord.

Well, anyway, that's how we felt in September and October. By December, reality has set in. The total of giving appears to be up over last year, but it is nowhere near what we had hoped. Disillusionment hangs over the heads of all persons who are suffering post-count'em depression.

Such a scenario does not necessarily mean that we ministers own up to the truth and face reality. We have a way of going repeatedly into denial when we interpret our congregation to our peers. Pride blinds perception. We want to look competent. We want to make it look as if we are serving a church that is thriving under our stellar leadership. We create our own illusions to paint as rosy a picture as we can to show that life is good in Old First Church. In fact, we go into full-stage fantasy when we tell our congregation about itself. We want our people to think they have one humdinger of a minister, so we create illusions rather than telling it like it is about the state of stewardship in our church.

We know how it works. Let's suppose that our five-hundred members represent 250 families or households. Since 250 numbers would be far too cumbersome for us to tally here, let's take a representative 10 percent segment of the 250 households. These twenty-five families have pledged in a distribution that is identical to the church as a whole. Of the twenty-five, six have refused to turn in a card at all. Two turned in a card with zero written on it. The other pledges break down as follows:

Amount Pledged Per Year

$ 78
104
156
260
260
360
360
520
520
780
1,000
1,000
1,200
1,560
1,800
2,600
4,000

These pledges total $16,558, 10 percent of the $165,580 pledged for next year's ministry and mission. We discover that this pledge number is 6 percent higher than the total pledged in the campaign last year. Then we sit at our desks and spin the giving statistics so we can portray how beautifully everything is going under our brilliant leadership. We decide to come up with the average pledge as a sign of our church's health. Of course we will elect not to count the households that did not send in a pledge card. We rationalize that we want an average only of pledges that were received. Then, of course, we will argue to ourselves that we should not include persons who pledged zero because zero is really not a pledge. So we decide that the $16,558 total of the cards should be divided by seventeen actual pledges. This allows us to claim to parishioners and public alike that in our church people pledge on average $974. More likely we'll round it up and proudly announce, "In my church the average pledge is up over last year to around a thousand dollars per household." Then we smile smugly as we wait for accolades. We braggers always use averages.

Realists use medians. Realists look at all the households of the church and seek that median household commitment right in the center of the church. Since we have an even number of 250, there is really no one household that is absolutely in the middle. To make it simpler, since our 10 percent sampling is an odd number, 25, we can pinpoint exactly the median. It will be household number 13 in the hierarchy of giving. Exactly 12 families give more and exactly 12 families give less. Now remember that 6 households did not respond at all and 2 sent in a big fat goose egg. That takes care of eight (8) households. Then we remember that one household pledged $78 (9), another pledged $104 (10), another $156 (11) and still another $260 (12). These are the lowest 12 households in our sampling. The median household will be household number 13, which also is a pledge of $260 for the Lord's work. If we want an honest look at the giving level of the congregation, it is not the fabricated average of $974 (almost $1,000) that we boast about. It is in reality $260 a year, because half of the congregation is giving more than that and half of the congregation is giving less.

Whenever a stewardship committee shares the amount of the average pledge, however dishonestly calculated, people seem to nod that it sounds about right to them. When, however, the committee takes time to calculate the median household gift, beware. The congregation will gasp in disbelief when this number is shared. I once dropped this number in a sermon in a wealthy parish in a wealthy community, and received a death threat the following week. Church folk do not like to be faced with the median number, which is (in most instances) frighteningly low. In point of fact, most of us in the ministry don't like to face that harsh median number reality either.

Numerous church leaders have made the embarrassing point that if all the households in a typical mainline denominational church had an income just below the poverty line and they tithed (10 percent of income to the church), the annual budget of our churches would go up astronomically. If the median household in the Church of St. Smythes' happened to be tithers, that means their median annual income is $2,600. Yeah, right. Or if the average pledge (among pledgers) in the church represents a tithe, the average annual income is $9,740. Believe that and I'll sell you some beachfront property in Nebraska.

I once interviewed a search committee from a wonderful church. They were a fine group of people. They rather liked to be on the cutting edge. They liked to be relevant. They liked to be doing new things in novel ways. Naturally they wanted to know where I stood on certain issues. They wanted to know whether or not I had the courage to get into the pulpit and say anything that was controversial. I allowed as how my style was usually to do the controversial things through committees and the session. However, yes, I would not be afraid to get into the pulpit and blast forth with a controversial sermon from time to time. They seemed to like that and leaned forward in their chairs a little bit, thinking that maybe they had a live one on the line.

They wanted to know whether I would have the courage to be sufficiently controversial that some people might get upset. In an odd way they seemed to want that. I could say quite honestly, "Yes, there have been moments when I have preached a controversial sermon and people have become terribly upset. In fact, some people have left our church and joined another congregation because of a stand I have taken in the pulpit." That really thrilled them. So I went on to regale them with stories of threats to my personal safety. By now the committee was loving me.

One of them inquired, "Could you tell us what was the most controversial sermon you ever preached?" They wondered what the issue was. Was it the abortion issue? Was it gay rights? Was it a challenge to patriotism? What was the most controversial sermon I ever delivered?

I said, "Oh, yes, I can remember that very easily. It was indeed after that sermon that I got the most seething venom hurled my way." "Oh, tell us," they pleaded. "What was the most controversial sermon you ever preached?" I said, "It was the Sunday I looked the congregation in the eye and told them that they should give at least 10 percent of their income to the work of the church." With that the air went out of the committee's balloon. Clearly they were losing interest in my candidacy as their possible minister. They quickly changed the subject to more polite matters. You see, that topic was even too controversial for them.

Do you hear what these people were saying? Give us any controversial subject you want. Stir us up. Challenge us. Get way out front on the issues, but don't dare invade our lives where personal commitment lives. Don't mess with our wallets.

We could list many other aspects of the church's life besides attendance and giving that would testify to a lack of commitment. Rather than raise our blood pressure any farther, let's just say that parish ministry is not often done among a membership that is wholly dedicated to serving the Lord. Yes, our morale is lifted when we encounter those parishioners who are saints. They have a faith that is alive. They are an inspiration. Still other members are close to what one might call commitment. They are growing in their faith. Still others among our membership are honestly seeking a living faith. There are plenty of positives that need to be noted. It is just that the hard truth of parish life is such that far too many, if not the majority, of parishioners show little to no commitment to serving our Lord, and give little evidence of wanting to change.

Whether we are able to sustain a ministry and serve the Lord with faithful effectiveness depends in no small way on how we handle and react to our own disillusionment.

If we would faithfully serve the Lord and continue in this calling, it is mandatory that we bear two things in mind. The first is to know that we are not alone. Our church at St. Smythes is quite typical. We may not believe that, listening to our fellow pastors. They tell us stories about their churches that make us feel that we must be hopeless incompetents to have such a low-commitment congregation. We must be failures. We wonder if we should leave the parish ministry.

We need to be let in on the deep, dark secret. We clergy are highly skilled liars when we talk to each other. Our colleagues are so good at offering bogus numbers that we believe them. We should instead remember that they too are in denial, because still other clergy have lied to them and made them feel inferior, afraid to face the truth about the congregations they serve. They are spewing out their denial numbers to us, and we are quietly comparing their denial numbers to our real numbers and feeling hopelessly put down. We end up countering with our denial numbers, and go home feeling awful.

We need to find a fellowship of pastors with whom we can be honest. When we are honest and vulnerable, we discover the truth that we are not alone. We are a fellowship of pastors with a common uphill battle.

Secondly, let's see before us not a sign of failure, but a mission field of opportunity. The five-hundred names on the roll joined that church at some point for largely good reasons. They were seeking. They wanted to express their faith. They wanted to be a part of the church of Jesus Christ. For many of them that faith has not taken root in their lives as they hoped it would. Life is difficult, and it takes its toll. Many have sensed that their faith has slipped away. The congregation to which we are called is one of the most challenging mission fields on the face of the earth. God has called us to be a minister in this place, faithfully, patiently nurturing our parishioners, confronting them with the biblical truth, praying for them, loving them, visiting them. Day in and day out, week in and week out, we model for them what the Christian walk is all about.

The present-day church of Jesus Christ in North America has a massive commitment problem. The good news is that it does not have to stay that way. Renewal can occur. The best response to our disillusionment is not denial or bitterness or resignation. It is a rekindling of our call and embarking on faithful service.

Chapter 19

Knowing What People Give

We are guaranteed a good debate if we raise the issue of whether the minister should know what people give to the church. Not long ago a magazine stirred up quite a bit of interest when a columnist wrote that a minister should know what people give. He gave as one of his rationales the fact that the only way Jesus knew that the widow had given a mite to the Temple was obviously that he knew what she gave. Letters to the editor flowed in opposition. Several of the letter writers apparently bought into the dubious homiletical notion that a passage of Scripture can have only one meaning. They argued that making a point of Jesus' knowing what the widow gave was to miss the primary thrust of the passage, which was another point altogether. Therefore, one cannot use this passage to defend knowing what people give. Lost in all that convoluted erudition is the simple fact that, of course, he knew.

A better argument against knowing what people give might be taken from that portion of the Sermon on the Mount where Jesus advises his followers to give their alms in secret.

> Beware of practicing your piety before others in order to be seen by them; for then you have no reward from your [God] in heaven.
> So whenever you give alms, do not sound a trumpet before you, as the hypocrites do in the synagogues and in the streets, so that they may be praised by others. Truly I tell you, they have received their reward. But when you give alms, do not let your left hand know what your right hand is doing, so that your alms may be done in secret; and your Father who sees in secret will reward you. (Matt. 6:1–4)

One might argue that for the sake of preserving the secrecy our Lord wants, we dare not expose parishioners' giving records even to ourselves.

Certainly the public at large is more comfortable in the belief that we do not know. Now, at the beginning of a new century, money is our obscenity. Money matters are considered to be a person's private domain—none of our business—don't ask, don't tell. My money is for me to know and for you not to find out. While many people seem to have no problem showcasing the fruits of wealth, and published reports do make known the salaries of athletes, entertainers, and executives, we know that it is downright gauche to ask a person how much she brings home in her paycheck. Quizzing her about what percentage of her resources she gives to charity is an unforgivable social blunder. So how dare the preacher pry into people's private lives to find out who gives what to the church?

Something there is that does not like a snoop and looking into people's money, and looking at giving seems like snooping. So the momentum is strong that we should leave mediocre enough alone and not pry where we don't belong. We should not know what people give.

Ironically, it is the argument that I hear most often from colleagues who refuse to know what their parishioners give that sets up my reasons for believing it is quite valuable for our ministries when we do indeed know what folks give. My sisters and brothers argue thusly: "A minister should not know what people give so that said minister will not be influenced by money." The supposition, I guess, is that stewardship resembles a political fund-raiser. Give $1,000 and you are invited in to the dinner. Give $10,000 and you get to attend a private party before the dinner. Give $100,000 and you sit down with the candidate for a personal chat after the dinner.

A constant concern in any church family is that we the clergy might play favorites. Of course, we have friends. Human nature being what it is, there will inevitably be hurt feelings among some people who resent our close friendships with certain other parishioners. While we regret these hurt feelings, we accept them as an inevitable trade-off that comes from our leading as normal a life as we can.

However, when the pastor appears to cozy up to the big-money people because they are big money people, the congregation's respect for us is legitimately lowered. After all, Scripture is quite clear:

> My brothers and sisters, do you with your acts of favoritism really believe in our glorious Lord Jesus Christ? For if a person with gold rings and in fine clothes comes into your assembly, and if a poor person in dirty clothes also comes in, and if you take notice of the one wearing the fine clothes and say, "Have a seat here, please," while to the one who is poor you say, "Stand there," or, "Sit at my feet," have you not made distinctions among yourselves, and become judges with evil thoughts? Listen, my beloved brothers and sisters. Has not God chosen the poor in the world to be rich in faith and to be heirs of the kingdom that he has promised to those who love him? But you have dishonored the poor. Is it not the rich who oppress you? Is it not

they who drag you into court? Is it not they who blaspheme the excellent name that was invoked over you? (James 2:1–7)

Any time we find ourselves putting our private lives and our public ministries for sale by giving favored treatment to the rich just because they are rich, we need to take some time off and reexamine our motives. When colleagues insist that we should never know what people give lest we be tempted to show favoritism, their intention is worthy. They sense they could be tempted to practice what is condemned in the letter of James.

Unfortunately, the strategy neither addresses the issue nor solves the problem. The issue is being influenced by money. The issue is showing favoritism toward rich people in a way that disobeys Scripture and sells out our integrity. The issue is sinfulness.

The truth is that we clergy are much more thoroughly sinful than we might want to admit. We are as fallen as everybody else. Let's not be naive. While we might wish we could live in a world where closing our eyes to stewardship information would cleanse us from the sin of being unbiblically influenced by money, we do not live in that world. We live in the real world, where a person whose judgment is corrupted by money will inevitably have his or her judgment corrupted by money. Period. We cannot escape our sin, nor can we escape being influenced by money. I do not like making a disparaging remark about colleagues, but let's be honest: Anyone who believes he or she can avoid being unbiblically influenced by money by refusing to look at giving information is hopelessly dull-witted.

One afternoon I sat in the front seat of a hearse (if I must be in a hearse, I prefer to be among those sitting up and talking). The funeral director got in and sat behind the wheel. While we waited for the signal that the procession was ready to go, a large, expensive car crossed in front of us and pulled into one of the few available parking spaces, clearly marked "For church use only." A dignified-looking gentleman got out of the car, saw me in the hearse, waved, and nonchalantly walked out of the parking area, away from the church, and out onto the main street. Whatever his business happened to be that day, it did not involve church, except to occupy a "For church use only" parking space.

The funeral director slapped the steering wheel and laughed. "How about that guy. You can't do much about that, can you? It's guys like that who pay the bills around your place. You have to let him be as rude as he wants to be." The illegal parker was well known as a member of our church.

He was also a well-known leader in the business community. He and his wife lived in a large house just south of town, a place they had called home for several decades. Over the years they had developed a significant reputation for being powerful people. They sat on boards. They belonged to clubs. He occupied the front corner office of a respected company in the community. Everyone knew he was something of a blowhard, but they put up with it because "he is like that." Besides, people like to be graced by the moneyed and powerful, however rough the edges.

He was a man who spoke with authority around the church. If he wanted to see me, various people in the hallways would escort him to my office, breaking in on whatever I might be doing so that Mr. So-and-so could say, "Hi." If word got out that he disapproved of something the church was doing, people quaked in their loafers.

Reflecting on the awe in which the funeral director and people around the church held this man, it became clear that being unbiblically influenced by money has nothing to do with what a person gives to church. The funeral director did not have any idea what if anything the man gave. The people who scurried down the hallways to open doors for him to barge into my office had no idea. All they knew was that the man had a prominent, very-well-paying position. He had an expensive house and car. He belonged to expensive clubs. He and his wife sat on boards that expect generous contributions from their members. He appeared to have "gold rings" and "fine clothes," and it was quite naturally, though unbiblically, assumed that he and his wife should have the finest seats in the church and illegal parking privileges in our church lot.

Every pastor has heard the refrain and even joked about it. The captain of industry moves to town. The biggest house in the neighborhood has new owners. The professional family with expensive sports cars arrives on the scene. Haven't we all heard it? "I wonder what their religious affiliation is." "Those are the kinds of people we want in the church." People come to us on the q.t. and hint that they might be able to set up a meeting for us to get to know "the family in the big house." Then parishioners urge us on to land the big fish. "They'll give a boost to the budget."

The whole ethos of our church life is quite easily infected by an unbiblical chasing after rich people. Not knowing what people give in no way exempts us from the game. In fact, it may make us more vulnerable.

After many years in the pastorate, I am convinced that being sinfully influenced by money is much more insidiously a part of our ministries than we want to admit. It is often part of a largely unconscious game our church plays with us. Part of the reason that some members of the church family do not want us to know what they give has nothing to do with our being unbiblically influenced by money. These people may be more spiritually savvy than we are. They may know that we are fallible, sinful folk who are susceptible to being swayed by money. They just don't want us to be influenced by what they *give*.

They are much more comfortable when they think that we are influenced by what they *have*. That is how they believe the world responds to them, and they have learned to appreciate the church's relating to them the same way.

The man who drove his expensive car into a church parking space had money. That was all he needed us to know. By having money he assumed and appropriated more than his share of advantages around the church, as he did at the club and around town.

Did you notice in the passage from James that there is no mention of what people give? All that is mentioned is that one person is rich while another is poor. The sin that James highlights is favoring those who have, while ignoring those who have not. Alas, we in church have not done well in our ministry to the haves and have-nots. We routinely cozy up to the haves. Nothing out of the ordinary about that, sad to say. When a church member welcomes a shabbily dressed have-not, we have a story that finds its way into devotional guides and pops up repeatedly in our e-mail. Hobnobbing with the poor is news.

Let's take it a step farther. We have all read stories of a spinster schoolteacher who lived in a small, run-down house. She had only one dress and she bought very sparse amounts of food for herself. Then she died at age ninety-five, leaving 1.7 million dollars to her college. She was rich. She had it, but nobody knew it.

Haven't we read statistics about some of the families buying the huge mansions? They are so in over their heads with mortgage payments, school tuitions, car payments that they are poor. One wrong move, a lost job, and they will have to declare bankruptcy.

In many instances life in America is like a poker game. We don't know who's holdin' and who's bluffin'.

I do not really know if the man in the big car was as securely rich as we all figured or if his accounts were running thin. I don't know if he was sending money to help his kids or if his kids were sending money to help him. All the funeral director and I knew for sure was that he had one boat of a car, his clothing was upper crust, and his house would fetch a small fortune were he to sell it. I could not testify under oath whether he was really rich or really on the verge of having to sell it all and live off the kids. In other words, the funeral director and countless members of the church catered to the man not because he was rich. They did not know for sure about that. They catered to him because of his conspicuous consumption, which they did know about because it was, well, conspicuous.

If we are not careful, and if we are not sensitive to our own sinfulness and the sinfulness of our congregation, we will quite easily drift into a terribly unbiblical quagmire. In a world where money talks, the leadership of our churches will get into the hands of the wrong people. Instead of seeing the spiritually gifted and authentically committed souls in positions of authority, our churches will be taken over by conspicuous consumption. The millionaire retired schoolteacher will be passed over because she does not conspicuously consume. The extravagant couple in debt over their heads to pay for their mansion, sports cars, and fine clothing will be asked to be church officers because they conspicuously consume. Such is the inevitable consequence of "not being biblically influenced by money." Such is the inevitable consequence of being naive about our own sinfulness. Such, I believe, is the sad consequence of not knowing what people give.

As I sat in that hearse and listened to the funeral director go on about how that man with the big car paid our church's bills, I knew that the man for all his supposed wealth gave $300 a year to the church. He had given the same amount every year for years. I also knew that the janitor in the man's office building, who was a church member as well, gave $850 a year. Since in most instances the guy with the office window makes more per year than the guy who empties his wastebasket, it was a short mental leap for me to reason that the janitor was giving a much higher percentage of his earnings to the work of Jesus Christ through our church than his boss was. Since I am convinced that Halford Luccock was correct when he said that the best way to discover what people really believe is to look at their check stubs, I came to understand that the janitor was a more faithful disciple of Jesus Christ than was the well-tailored chap whose office he cleaned. Now when in the halls of the church the two men each voiced an opinion, who do you suppose I listened to more intently? I listened to the janitor, not because he appeared sociologically to be poor compared to the other man's apparent riches, but because he showed himself in his giving to be faithful and the other man did not. Armed with info from the financial office, I could see what I might ordinarily have missed. In their personalities, one was a generous servant; the other was a conspicuous consumer, a tightwad, and a bully.

To say that any of us is never influenced by money is to be naive and probably to tell an out-and-out lie. Money talks. The question is whether we will be biblically or unbiblically influenced. It has been necessary for me to have access to giving records so that my ministry can stand over against the tendency to be unbiblically bullied by the apparently well-to-do. Our ministries need to be based on the simple truth—quite obvious when you think about it—that the local church should be led by the Christians and not by the conspicuous consumers.

Some caveats and observations:

1. Realizing our sinfulness, we need to be constantly reminding ourselves that our pastoral care and all aspects of the church's ministry are open to all.

There is no financial prerequisite for singing in the choir, working on a mission project, or receiving a hospital visit.

2. The gross dollar amount of giving can tell us who is helping the church budget. It is not a definitive indicator of spiritual commitment. Back to the story of the widow's mite. We assume the rich folk were lobbing higher amounts into the coffers than she was. Gross amount was not what caught Jesus' attention. Her gift was a higher percent of her net worth and was thus spiritually more important. For this reason, if the captain of industry giving $4,000 a year gets upset, we have a political problem that we can hopefully handle through some appropriate management technique. If an elderly person living in a one-room apartment over a drugstore, having only a bed, a dresser, and a hot plate and giving $3.28 a week, gets mad at us, we have a spiritual problem that will require time, patience, careful listening, and much prayer.

3. If every member of the church family were asked to list the top ten givers in the congregation, no one would get it right. No one would even be close.

4. I can be influenced by money. I admit it. That is why I need to know what people give, so I can be influenced biblically rather than fall into the trap of being influenced unbiblically. I want to be influenced by people whose giving shows they are serious about their faith. I do not want to be influenced by people whose giving shows little to no commitment at all. This is a very rough concept. But I believe the Christians should have the most influence in the church.

5. People assume they are typical. The tightfisted assume that the congregation will respond to a new idea in a tightfisted way. Persons who tithe figure most people tithe. An idea to develop a new program will thus tend to be opposed by most of the tightfisted because they cannot believe that the church would lend its support. The tithers say, "Go for it. We'll find the money."

6. It has been my experience that a disproportionately high percentage of generous givers are very supportive of mission. They are disproportionately willing to take risks to expand mission. The less generous are more likely to see a balanced budget as akin to the kingdom of God. Generous givers are more likely to believe the Lord will provide if we venture forth in trust. After all, that is what they themselves are doing in their large financial support.

Each pastor must resolve this question in his or her own ministry. Faithful ministries are carried on by persons who come down on either side of the fence on this issue. I have found that having access to financial records has provided most helpful guidance in the battle to keep the church from being taken over by conspicuous consumption. I have also found myself leaning on the influence of the generous. They inspire me to be more prophetic. They lead me to become more mission-driven. They witness to what it is to trust the Lord. Why not be influenced by givers?

Chapter 20

The Mission Committee

*I*t is not at all uncommon to arrive at a church and find that mission has been relegated to the shadows. Few people are talking about it. No hunger to get on with the business of tackling expanded mission work can be heard growling in the congregation's inner being. In fact, one can spend many days snooping around the building without having the slightest inkling that this church has any mission program at all.

Then it crops up on the calendar: Mission committee meeting, 7:30 P.M., conference room. Pray for strength, patience, and a pastor's heart before attending this one. Our first impression on entering the meeting will be that very few people are there, maybe four or five. We had no idea how many to expect, because no one we could find knew who served on this committee, and no minutes of previous meetings could be found. Not knowing who to call for information about such things as a list of names, we have to show up cold.

Our second impression is that we came on the wrong night or wandered into the wrong room. This has to be a twelve-step program for abused people. They are glum, apparently having had all semblance of emotion drained from them by one put-down after another.

Nonetheless, there is a determined martyrdom to their demeanor. They are there because they are "dedicated." Their grimness is a sign that they have persevered, fought the good fight, represented the faithful remnant in an otherwise comfortable club of a congregation. Hence our entrance is met with no high fives or toothy "glad to see ya" grins. They acknowledge that we have appeared, while looking at us with wary eyes, trying to figure out if we are a real disciple who will join them in being marginalized by "the powers that be around here," or whether we are a slick politician who will pander to the "big shots," bless their heathen lifestyles, while abusing and stepping on the mission committee.

This promises to be a long evening.

When, just after 11 P.M., the meeting adjourns having made no decisions about anything, we leave with further insights into St. Smythes'. The mission committee understands mission exclusively in financial terms. It is money "we don't spend on ourselves; we send it to others." Mission boils down to a budget, which we easily compute to be slightly less than 10 percent of the congregation's total expenses. One committee tried to put a good spin on it by feigning a boast that this was almost a tithe.

What strikes us is that, for a rather small budget, a tremendous number of "missions" are listed. Several of those missions are getting no more than $100 a year. Apparently, members of the church have lobbied for their pet service projects, and the mission folks have not wanted to alienate the givers by refusing their requests. Even if the person having recommended a project has died or moved to another state, the agency keeps getting $100 a year. "They've come to depend on us." Yea, right.

Denominational mission giving is right in there with the visiting nurses, the YMCA, and a young lady from the next town who is at a faraway campus representing Youth for Christ. "They are so committed and doing such important work with young people, you know." For all we can tell, the mission committee sees itself as a very pale version of the United Way. The only difference is that the United Way has confidence and is very public in its drive for success. The mission committee has no confidence in its private settling on failure.

We should not overlook the fact that a high number of congregations harbor only a small cadre of souls who claim they want to support mission. Unfortunately, these folks have received little support or encouragement from the rest of the church family. Perhaps some years ago they tried to get a large increase in mission giving. The way they tell it, at first everybody seemed excited. Minutes for mission, posters, bulletin inserts, the whole nine yards went into interpreting mission that year. Alas, once the pledges were counted and the budget was honed to fit fiscal reality, the mission budget was reduced to what it had been the year before. Then to rub salt in the wound, in December when it became obvious the income was not what the trustees had hoped, the last quarter's mission budget allotments were not paid at all.

The next year the committee proposed only a 5 percent increase, provided it would all be paid. They got a 1 percent increase, and 10 percent of that total was never paid.

Since then these same people have seen no reason to propose anything new. It only made the treasurer mad when they did. They figure any hoopla about mission interpretation wouldn't do any good anyway. Of course, mission will be cut to balance the budget, and then not fully paid. Year after year these committee stalwarts have seen it as their job to be the last bastion of caring in an uncaring religious club. Now they are burned out, worn out, beaten up, fed up, and resigned to the hopelessness of being victims in defense of mission.

Hearing their testimonies of despair and then watching the money gurus actually cut into mission, just as these mission folks said, we empathize with them. They have come by their hopelessness the old-fashioned way. They have earned it.

Arriving on the scene, we have the task of rendering a diagnosis. It is for us to recognize that the symptoms just laid out before us indicate an illness, which needs to be cured.

The first step is to make sure that the congregation understands its denominational identity. What this means will vary from denomination to denomination. In the Presbyterian Church the budget is set by the session. They can follow any number of processes leading up to their setting of the budget, but the bottom line is that session is the final court of appeals for prioritizing the expenditure of money. Denominational rules matter, because in too many churches a cult of financial pruners have overstepped their bounds, usurping the authority of what is supposed to be the congregation's ruling body.

These financial people are a tremendous help to any church, and not infrequently keep the church from fiscal lunacy. Their gift of administration is a blessing. The problem is that all too often they are so driven by ledger statements and bottom lines that they fail to appreciate mission. Mission, after all, does not have a conspicuous financial payoff for us. It is viewed by the treasurer's office as a giveaway. Since financial types are not usually mission people, we need to do some shifting of who holds the reigns of power. By reaffirming that budget decisions are the province of the ruling board, we not only put money matters where they ultimately belong; we also put them in a setting that is far more likely than a trustee meeting to give a sympathetic ear to the task of moving the church into mission.

The second step is more difficult and less naturally faced. That is the step of realizing that the biggest barrier to mission in the local congregation is very often the mission committee itself. These seemingly dedicated symbols of perseverance have become so accustomed to having their budget cut and their commitments unpaid that they have resigned themselves to failure. Sad to say, in many instances the committee members have crossed a fateful line. It is not uncommon for us to find a mission committee that in practice seems more committed to failure than to leading a congregation into mission.

They live out the self-fulfilling prophecy. They quietly propose a budget increase that is negligible. They do not bother to single out any projects to be highlighted as having special urgency. In fact, they offer the congregation no specific mission program and no urgency at all.

Then during the year, instead of celebrating where mission payments are going, instead of letting the congregation in on what is happening as it happens, mission work is done in the private inner sanctum of the financial office. Checks will be written, and no one will be told about it.

If during the year a significant need arises, little is done to respond. Special offerings are frowned on. Someone got the idea that these offerings dilute stewardship. On top of that, there are virtually no unbudgeted funds in our budget to allow for flexibility. As a result, when the budget has been set everyone assumes the church is not allowed to have any new creative responses for the next twelve months. So if a fire takes out a row of houses in the parish, the church feels it has no way to respond. "Our budget is set. We don't have extra money. We don't take special offerings. We'll pray for the victims, but send no funds."

Longtime mission committee members likely harbor a latent resentment of the church. By their lack of positive interpretive messages to the congregation, they may unintentionally be setting the church up for failure, the payoff being that they are able to render a harsh judgment of other parishioners. The script they have written for themselves is that "we are the faithful martyrs in an unfaithful church." By the time we arrive on the scene the mission committee members may well have become so wedded to this script that we will meet irrational resistance if we try to change their character in a way that will either recast them in a role other than martyr or the congregation in any role other than unfaithful church.

Hard as it is to say, to the extent that the mission committee demonstrates any or all of these admittedly caricatured traits, we are required to look on them as more an impediment for mission enhancement than a help. Our task is to help everyone, including the mission committee, reimagine what this congregation really is. Returning to the image of the church as a massive family reunion, the larger family milling around under the tent would love to be helpful to others. That's right; they would. They would respond generously to a clear challenge to do mission. They need guidance, specific steps to follow, specific needs to which they can respond. They will warm to the idea of becoming a family that draws its identity from the good that it does. The family has not taken those steps in mission largely because the particular group of cousins, aunts, and uncles who have taken mission as their province are not letting the rest of the kin in on it.

We should never put all our hopes on the mission committee to be the instigator of revitalized mission. I have seen a woman's group take the lead. I have seen youth take the lead. I have seen ad hoc task forces take the lead. I have yet to arrive in a church where the existing mission committee was playing a leading role. So I don't look first to the mission committee to jump-start mission.

Though the mission committee has seen mission almost exclusively as giving money, and is down in the dumps because the church gives so little, we will be shocked to find that said committee rises up to oppose us if we dare to propose that we increase the mission budget by 20 to 50 percent for next year. They have had too many dreams shattered already. Of course they don't want to be hurt again, but their excuse is, "Besides, we would need time to figure out how to use that much money."

We tell the mission committee of our intent, so they can't say they didn't know what we were about to do. Then we disregard their foot-dragging and go unilaterally to the ruling board with our proposal. In many churches there is more chance of getting the ruling board to go for an increase in mission than of having healed enough wounds to get a positive response from the mission committee.

Then when the stewardship numbers are in and the cutting knife is out, we fight tooth and nail to get as sizable an increase in mission as possible. We dig in and insist we cut other lines of the final budget before we cut mission. Members of the mission committee are in complete disbelief. They are shaken. They are thrilled. Their world is being reordered.

We should not be surprised if a few members of the committee see this as their time to step off the committee. They suddenly feel their fatigue. It is indeed time to let them go, with our gratitude for having taken shrapnel for as long as they have. They limp away, having done their job about as well as it could have been done under the circumstances.

The congregation is informed of the increase and thanked for their support. How good it is to have taken a step toward becoming a mission church!

Then we get the ruling board to take a further step in integrity. We will honor our mission commitments come hell or high water. Working with the trustees and treasurer, we will monitor income to plan that mission goals are met, even if other vital programs must be cut or we must fail to balance the books at the end of the year. A vote by the ruling board to lock in our commitment to pay mission even at the risk of not balancing the year-end budget is a giant step forward.

Then during the year we agree to receive special offerings. For some reason, some churches are allergic to special offerings. Of course special offerings can be overdone, and can begin to undermine the annual stewardship campaign. In moderation, some special offerings can do wonders. An earthquake in Central America, a flood in Africa, a refugee crisis in Eastern Europe,

a house fire in our community or a nearby city—all of these are specific catastrophes involving specific people, where our dollars can go precisely to do
some good. We will rarely see such a need put before our people and not have
them respond generously according to their means. Announcing the total
offering sent, announcing the good we have done, drives home the message
that we are a mission church that responds to need.

As the Smythe family sees what it can do, a few people will rejoice, "It's
about time." They will say, "How can I participate?" The mission committee
begins to have new faces at the table. We might even consider assigning more
members from the ruling board as well as from the congregation at large to
the committee. New blood is fresh blood, and the committee begins to come
alive.

It is time to start to look for that one local project that will define mission
for the whole church family. Over the course of my ministry it has taken the
form of a dialogue with storefront academies in Harlem, a migrant ministry,
a senior citizens project, a building rehab project, a health insurance program
for children, an interaction with an urban neighborhood. When the church
family has a name it can hang on mission, it becomes even more involved.

Mission trips are a great way to introduce people to the international scene.
Youth trips, adult trips, and trips by doctors or other professionals to lend their
talents to the world stage all bring back stories of what God is doing in far-
off places. The testimonies of what the trip has done to change the lives of
those who went will excite the church.

Of course, we do need to hold a few principles in mind for the sake of pre-
venting our church's enthusiasm from self-destructing.

1. New people signing on provide an excellent opportunity for education
in how congregations are organized. The new people cannot let their enthusiasm send them chasing off with no accountability to anyone. The newly invig-
orated mission committee needs to be told at the beginning and again as often
as possible that they serve at the will of the ruling board, With the concurrence
of the ruling board, their task is to help unleash and coordinate the mission
outreach of the whole congregation. They are to report to the board at each
regularly scheduled meeting, helping them to understand and support mission
work. You would be surprised how difficult it is to get mission people to do
this.

2. As excited people get together, conflicts can emerge between those who
are turned on by overseas mission and those who want all mission to be local.
At one special meeting to hash out just this conflict, we went around the room
and let people share their mission experience. Persons who had thought mission had to be local were brought to tears by the stories told of poverty and

disease in the third world. The committee began to experience how big mission is. They discovered that mission is rarely either/or. It is usually both/and and even more. An evening of sharing can build a team, helping people see how important it is to help each other.

3. Maybe it is time to look at the mission committee's organization. When five people met each month to read correspondence and whine about a budget that had not changed much in a decade, one did not need to fuss with the organization. Five people around a table once a month could pretty well handle the correspondence and the whining without added help.

Now that the work is growing, it might be time to ask some people to concentrate on the local mission projects, others to work with overseas mission and mission trips, others to screen potential mission projects, others to interpret mission to the congregation. The organizational model will vary from church to church. Sticking with the old model of everyone in one group meeting once a month usually causes folks to feel so much is on their plate that they do not have time to deal with even a fraction of the work before them. By splitting the work, we allow committee people to focus on a specific area and get more done.

4. The mission committee should be asked to dream. What would we do if the mission budget doubled and twice as many people volunteered to do mission? After a few years, people can begin to suspect that thinking big is not such an outrageous idea. They begin to think big automatically.

5. At some point we need to tackle the issue of denominational mission support. Left to themselves, a high percentage of mission committees and ruling boards will not be enthralled with denominational giving. Some will say they don't want to support an anonymous bureaucracy. Others will tick off a list of things any mainline denomination could have done that have gotten under their skin. Still others will say that mission is for us to do in the local church our own way, in a manner that suits our people. A few of us clergy can even catch ourselves teaching an antidenominational message because we feel such a tactic will help rally the troops while boosting our popularity.

If we take seriously Paul's analogy of the church being the body of Christ, we realize that not only can no one individual claim to be the body of Christ, no congregation can claim to be the fullness of it either. We all need to be challenged by a voice from beyond us, as Paul's voice challenged the Corinthians. We need to coordinate our mission with other churches, as Paul called on the Corinthians to do (2 Cor. 8–9).

As American society has become a vast collection of ghettos—some inner city, some suburban, some rural—we in the church are called to find ways to be in touch with churches in communities different from our own in order to see the immensity of God's love and God's work. The suburban stomach cannot say to the inner-city heart or the rural backbone, "I have no need of you." A denominational church makes the body of Christ feasible in our day and adds integrity to how we do mission. If nothing else, it reminds us that our immediate community is not all there is, nor is it the fullness of the kingdom of God. In Christ's plan we need to bump into each other and be made uncomfortable by the sharing of each other's hurts.

The most common question raised when we encourage denominational mission support is, "Why should we trust them?" My answer has been: For the same reason we ask the congregation to trust us. We are a prayerful gathering of people with diverse agendas trying to figure out together how best to allocate funds entrusted to us, to set priorities for these times, and to invite people to join us in mission. We are a microcosm of the denomination. There are people in this church who believe we've got it all wrong. There are people who cannot understand why we have decided as we have, yet we ask them to trust us. We model trust by supporting that megacongregation called the denomination.

Theologian Emil Brunner once said that the church exists by mission as fire exists by burning. Mission is that vital to our life together. The message of this section is that we often find ourselves called to a congregation where the poor souls on the mission committee have been beaten comatose by a long history of cutbacks, setbacks, and put-downs. To see mission come alive, we are well served not to look to that mission committee to play a lead role. Rather, it is our task to lead the ruling board and congregation into a vital expression of mission. This vital expression will then populate, invigorate, and propel the mission committee into mission.

Chapter 21

Spiritual Renewal for the Sake of Mission

*M*any historians believe that the legacy of the First Great Awakening was the American Revolution. In fact, documentation is available quoting several persons in England who dismissed the Revolution as merely a Presbyterian uprising.

Historians also argue that the Second Great Awakening led to the abolitionist movement and eventually the Emancipation Proclamation. Christians who had given their lives to Christ in the Second Great Awakening found that they could not both hold to their new faith and condone their old institution of slavery. They would not forsake their new faith. Slavery had to go.

There was not a social agenda on a front burner of either awakening. Both were primarily spiritual renewals. Yet each led quite clearly to social transformation. One can argue well into the night on the questions such as whether the Revolution and the abolitionist movement could have occurred without these spiritual awakenings. Wisdom would say that they probably would have happened. Few people could argue convincingly that they would have happened when they did, or as they did, without the impetus of the awakenings.

This lesson of history plays out in our ministries. We are very much in tune with God's rhythm when we make it a goal of our ministries to see spiritual renewal lead to mission. My own catchphrase is "Spiritual renewal for the sake of mission."

Do understand what I am *not* saying. We should never exploit spiritual renewal by suggesting it is merely a means to the end of building mission. Spiritual renewal is not a gimmick, nor is it merely a token. When the Holy Spirit invades a life and allows Jesus to set up residence at the center of that life, we are talking about something far too precious to be considered merely a technique to achieve something else. Spiritual renewal is an end in itself. We cannot predict exactly what our Savior will do in and through a particular person. The Lord has a marvelous uncontrollability. We certainly can never assume that spiritual renewal will issue in a particular social agenda, so we can never suggest that renewal is to be exploited to increase mission. About all we can say is that church history and the personal experience of this author come together to note an uncanny coincidence between people's being spiritually awakened and their generously giving themselves to the service of mission.

For this reason I have found it odd that so many church folks don't cotton to spiritual renewal. I find it downright peculiar the way folks committed to mission carry on about the ills of evangelism and being born again and life in the Holy Spirit.

When an idea floats that involves getting more involved in evangelism or spiritual renewal, voices of resistance are inevitably heard declaring that we cannot "back down from our mission agenda." Evidently these people have had bad experience with evangelism. Instead of seeing renewal as a seedbed for daring mission, they have witnessed it as a withdrawal from the public square, a retreat into privatized piety. They consequently argue that all evangelism and renewal are a thwarting of mission. In their minds, if you are pro-mission you must be anti-evangelism.

I was once told by a colleague that we could never have spiritual renewal as a goal for our congregation because it was not measurable. If you can't quantify it, it doesn't exist. Good grief!

My most common experience of resistance to spiritual renewal comes at a clergy gathering where the conversation goes something like this: "I just had a family in my church come into my office and announce that they had been born again." Immediately, the group gathers around as if our poor colleague had just announced the death of a close relative. "Oh, that's terrible news." "What are you going to do?" "If we can help you through the crisis, please let us know."

You see, a pastor's first reaction to someone who has just experienced a spiritual renewal is fear. We all know from experience that the newly turned on parishioner will now inevitably have an irrational exuberance. We could cope with that. More than likely this individual will want everyone in the church to have exactly the same irrational exuberance in exactly the same way. "I was a spiritual wasteland before my experience with the Lord. If you haven't had my experience you are, therefore, in a spiritual wasteland. So you must have what I have. What's wrong with this church that 'you' haven't been leading people to 'my' experience? I think this church is a wasteland."

Admittedly, I have used a caricature. But I suspect almost all of us in ministry see a familiar picture when we read the caricature. We can think of persons who have used their spiritual rebirth as an occasion to become bullies. We all know that such people become troublemakers for their pastors.

So, if we are going to have a ministry dedicated to the proposition that spiritual renewal leads to mission, we need to keep our eyes open at the "spiritual renewal" end of the equation. We need to test the spirits.

When there is an awakening, persons turned on by it are often accused by fellow members of being "subjective" in their faith. The accusers say, "Listen to them. They talk about *their* experience, what happened to *them*, how the Lord has touched *their* lives, and how it all feels to *them*." There is no dodging the evidence. Newly renewed people talk in the first person a lot.

We need to appreciate, however, the fact that when a person's life is spiritually remade that person is understandably overwhelmed by "what just happened in *my* life." Of course the testimony will be subjective and all about "*my*" experience. As John Newton put it in his great hymn: "Amazing grace, how sweet the sound, that saved a wretch like *me*! *I* once was lost, but now am found, was blind, but now *I* see" (italics mine). Newton's subjective renewal in God's grace led him to play a significant role in the abolition of slavery. Of course genuine renewal will have its subjective sound. Unless the Spirit gets into a person's life personally, how can there be commitment?

Alas, there is a not so fine a line between spiritual renewal that touches a person at the core of that person's being and the shallow turn-on of a "bless me club." We are dealing with an inexact science here, as spiritual detractors are fond of reminding us. Hard-and-fast rules are not to be found. Some general and necessarily vague standards should be held in the backs of our minds, nonetheless. While we admit that the Spirit is uncontrollable, there are potential patterns of behavior we nonetheless find troubling. We should grow concerned if the person claiming a renewal or born-again experience:

1. Continues for a long time to talk more about "me" than about "the Lord"
2. Uses "my experience" as *the* authority on who God is and how God acts in human history
3. Has a judgmental rather than gracious air about his or her witness
4. Is not open to the fullness of Scripture, particularly the teaching found in 1 Corinthians 12
5. Quickly translates the renewal to a political agenda (usually friendly to the right wing), will not let that agenda in any way be subservient to the lordship of Christ, and will then demand that others have to follow said agenda to be called Christian
6. Shows no sign of having denied self. Watch out when the renewal is little more than assertiveness training for an arrogantly sinful nature
7. Shows a belligerent unwillingness to heed any traditional authority
8. Shows no increase in giving
9. Ignores mission and social outreach

Hard as it is to say, there are occasions when spiritually turned-on people pose a real problem that does need to be contained. Through it all, we have to hope that our teaching about the body of Christ will have prepared the congregation for the onslaught of the selfishly renewed bullies among us.

Having said all that, let's remember that, sad to say, the fretting is about an occurrence that is all too rare. I am driven by an awareness that most of the churches we are called to pastor will amaze us with their blasé lack of spiritual commitment. We don't need to exhaust ourselves discerning the spirits if we cannot set our eyes on any spirit to discern. Our biggest challenge is not discerning spirits. Many of us opt to let sleeping churches lie. Dead churches are, after all, easier to manage.

If, on the other hand, we are tired of churches that lack commitment, we need to accept the thought that the road to being an alive church, committed to serving the Lord and doing mission, travels through spiritual renewal— complicated, convoluted, and conflicted as it is.

So we point back to the Great Awakenings. They were evangelical, partly charismatic spiritual renewals. The sequence of those significant outpourings was one of spiritual renewal issuing in dramatic, revolutionary moral reform. After the individual was converted, that individual banded together with other converted individuals to convert the society.

Let's not lock in too tightly on the renewal to mission sequence. We live in a fascinating time, on the cusp of a new moment when involvement in mission work itself can be the road to spiritual renewal. I am approached frequently by unchurched folks who ask to enter the door to faith through a social-outreach project. "Pastor, I'm not very religious. I wonder if you have something I could do to help the homeless." We live in a time when it is too simplistic to say that we convert the individual who will then band together with other converted individuals and change the culture. Today the act of doing missionary work can become itself a theater of spiritual renewal. We need to keep our eyes open to the searching soul whose involvement in mission can lead to the spiritual renewal that will make mission a life-giving passion and not just a volunteer project. Regardless, whether a mission project or an evangelism project is the first step, it is urgent that we live out a holistic ministry where, for all the caveats, spiritual renewal and mission are allowed to happen and feed each other.

I see my role as being wholly and admittedly unable to make renewal happen. I pray for it, but I know I cannot create it. The Lord creates it. All this is to say that you are reading the book of a pastor who has witnessed quite a bit of spiritual renewal in his ministry, but doesn't have the foggiest idea how it has happened. All your befuddled author knows is that any spiritual renewal worth a hoot is the Lord's doing. "Unless the Lord builds the house, those who build it labor in vain" (Ps. 127:1). My role is to be savvy in knowing how to minimize the probability that either the church or I will stifle the renewal when the Lord does create it. Your author can be as cautious, even cynical, as the next person when it comes to evangelism and renewal. I have seen more than my share of bogus "spiritual hot tubs for Jesus." Through it all I am still convinced that my role is to be a "yes" presence for spiritual renewal in the congregation. My task is to encourage before I critique. My role is to declare renewal innocent until proven guilty. My job is to keep doors open to any possibility that the Lord might be at work renewing a life.

Despite all my suspicions, I celebrate spiritual renewal as a mandatory component of commitment, mission, and generosity.

When the Holy Spirit rushed down on the disciples as described in Acts 2, one of the first results of that experience was a new economy. No longer did people guard their possessions with a miserly grip. Now they were other-centered. "What's mine is yours. If you have a need, I'll share with you." The early church was a revolutionary fellowship, wherein the entire membership, most of it destitute, had no material needs because the spiritual renewal of Pentecost revolutionized people's attitude toward money and sharing. Spiritual renewal and mission were inseparably bound from the birth of the church.

When we instinctively quell any sign of evangelism or spiritual renewal, we may be stepping on the Lord's work unawares. We may be cutting off the one source of hope we have that this congregation might be freed up to do mission, to give generously of themselves, to show a new level of commitment.

I am writing a great deal in the pages of this book about freeing up a congregation to take risks in faith. Often the greatest risk taker must be the pastor, who takes a chance that the person who claims to have been born again might just be the real deal. Sometimes we need to risk investing time in a person who senses personal renewal and needs guidance, so that together we can discern what it means. Our role is to risk celebrating signs of God's activity and to align ourselves with the renewed.

I offer three episodes. In the first, I was processing down the center aisle with our guest preacher of the day, singing the opening hymn, when he whispered to me that it was his intention to have an altar call at the close of his sermon. He hoped I didn't mind. With that we went our separate ways into the chancel.

It was too late to do anything about it. Of course, I had been set up. I fretted my way through the liturgy, introduced the preacher, and braced myself for what I figured would be a great experience for some worshipers who tended to like that sort of thing, and an outrage to others, who would never want something like that to happen in the church again and would want me to see to it that it never did happen again. They would demand to know, "How could you be so dumb as to bring a person like that to preach in the first place?"

Well, as it happened, the sermon was quite good. The altar call was done in an inviting way that did not divide the congregation between those who came forward and those who did not. When a goodly number did walk to the front, where they knelt in prayer, it seemed to be with the blessing of everyone in the room. I don't feel myself called to make such invitations, but I have to say that this was very well done.

What caught my attention was that every member of our ruling board who was in attendance came forward to commit or recommit his or her life to Jesus Christ. The real blessing was that I could see a difference in our next session meeting. Bickering and caution gave way to excited cooperation. The work God wanted to do through this congregation became a thrilling possibility. Over the next months we began to dream dreams. We began to have a vision of what we could do. Mission programming took off, with several remarkable ministries begun. Get this: I noticed that I now came home from session meetings so excited about what the church was doing that I could not get to sleep for *good* reasons. Can you believe it?

Our second example is a husband and wife who came to me following a Communion service. The old words of an old liturgy had been offered. The elements had been served by elders the traditional way. Nothing was added to the basic Presbyterian service. The husband spoke for both of them when he said, "Something happened to us when we took the bread and the cup. It was as if the Lord actually came into our lives. I think what has happened to us is what you would call being born again."

Working with this family, it became obvious that the Lord now moved dynamically in their lives. Soon thereafter, when the husband lost his job, the family increased their estimate of giving 300 percent. They said the Lord would provide. Evidently the Lord did provide, because the man found employment and his giving increased even more. The two of them reached out to college students, began a prison ministry, called on the church to take more seriously the needs of persons victimized by injustice. They were so turned on to mission that the rest of the congregation sometimes wished they would just shut up about it. Of course they did not shut up, and through their leadership we became a more mission-centered congregation.

The third example is a man who attended a Bible class taught by a woman of profound faith and insight. A Bible class, mind you, an old-fashioned Bible class. Nothing fancy. Rows of chairs facing a podium, students listening to a Sunday morning lecture. Something in what she said was evidently used by God to change this man's life. His casual churchianity exploded into a life of discipleship. When his estimate of giving came in with a 1,000 percent increase, the financial secretary called the family to say that they had obviously made a mistake and put the decimal point in the wrong place. Nobody increases by 1,000 percent. Nobody does . . . unless spiritual renewal has occurred. This family became committed to Bible study and prayer, and acted as spokespersons for a dramatically increased mission program.

When the church goes about being the church, the Lord has an opportunity to change people's lives. We can rest in the knowledge that renewal is the Lord's work. The Lord, in the Lord's timing and in the Lord's way, will provide. When the Lord moves, the commitment problem begins to be solved. That irrational, subjective exuberance might just be the Lord at work in a person so that a whole congregation might begin to wake up. For those of us not content with the low commitment levels we too often find in the church, we need to pray. We need to turn to the Lord. We need to open all the doors we can, so that spiritual renewal can issue in commitment to mission. When we sense that God is moving in people's lives, our most important work needs to be done. That is precisely the moment when we are called to keep the doors open.

Chapter 22

Money Follows Vision

I am reaching the age where I wish I could go back and start over in seminary and in the ministry. The one stipulation, of course, has to be that I would know then what I know now. Few of us would want to relive it just the way we did the first time around. If we could go back with even some of the wisdom we have accumulated over the years, we know we could come closer to doing it right.

In most aspects of ministry my desire would be to go back and live the second time with more courage than I had the first time. The first chapter of Joshua is a favorite for me because in it God is repeatedly telling Joshua to have courage. The theme is that we cannot take the promised land unless our faith gives us the courage to go for it. As I look back over the "almosts" of my ministry, I wish above all else that I had had more confidence, more courage. For me and for others, the sad fact is that coming in as an outsider to the Smythe family reunion makes us feel as if we are walking on eggs, constantly on trial. It has a way of sapping our courage, turning us into self-protecting cowards.

If I could start again, I wonder if I would have the chutzpah to do away with the annual stewardship campaign. Probably not. I could never have that much courage, even with three or four chances to begin anew. The campaign has just been too ingrained into the fabric of each of the particular congregations I have served. The church family has seen it as something we Smythes do. The battle to do away with it would probably be too upsetting to the bean counters among our fellowship, who could not tolerate the stress of beginning a year without seemingly secure numbers on the income side of the ledger.

We have all heard from pastors whose churches do not have pledge cards. They shame us with their anecdotal material of success after success. Their leaders prayerfully set the budget, which has line-item amounts for what monies will be required if the church is to do what it must do to be a faithful follower of the Lord. The congregation is then called on through the year to meet or exceed that budget. Remarkably, as the stories portray it, these churches rise to the occasion time and again. Their mission budgets are large. Their staffs are complete. Their churches are more spiritually alive. The obvious step is to do away with our annual plea for pledges and just get on with it.

If you have the courage to step out in faith in this way, you have my permission to skip to the Conclusion.

If not, I offer some seemingly bold ideas for us chickens to consider. Suspecting as I do that not having a pledge campaign is probably better than having one, yet being a congenital coward who is afraid to venture forth without the security blanket of financial commitments literally in hand, I try to carry out a stewardship campaign in a way that frees us, nonetheless, from what I realize is the "pledge trap." I work to include in our church life some of the freeing possibilities of a "faith budget," as if we had no stewardship cards at all. So, fellow cowards, let us reason together. Realizing that some churches have no stewardship cards and yet thrive and are fiscally responsible, we are forced to wriggle out of the "pledge trap" and think in whole new categories.

1. The vitality of a church, its mission, its program, and its spiritual growth will be determined in no small part by how it juxtaposes vision and money. Inevitably, one will be the servant of the other. When a stewardship campaign locks us into the "pledge trap," vision follows money, in a scenario we know well. Various committees and organizations submit their requests for next year's budget. The Christian education and personnel committees have put in a request for an added staff member to work with the young people. The mission committee has proposed that we begin a relationship with a congregation in the third world, funding part of a building project on the other side of the globe. Our stewardship campaign then sets out to "raise funds" so that we can support this vision.

Then what happens? The pledge cards come in. They are counted. It is like getting our blood work back from the lab. It is like tabulating the votes on election night. It is like the jury coming back in with its verdict. The pledges rule. Their number combined with an already-agreed-on number for other income sources will lock us into what we are allowed to do in the coming fiscal year. The congregation has rendered its judgment as to what will be permissible. With their pledges they have trapped us—the "pledge trap."

Everyone knows in a vision-follows-money congregation that whatever vision the church had pre-stewardship is but a pipe dream. It has no reality. Only the pledges will determine what is real. In too many of our churches vision follows money. Vision is squeezed to fit what the pledges have told us reality is.

No one is surprised when the budget line for a youth worker is erased completely. We might try to appease the Christian ed people by saying we could possibly hire a person for ten hours a week, or we might be able to start a full-time position only in the last third of the year, with the understanding that if next year's pledges are not adequate the person will be cut to part-time or let go. The mission project in the third world will not begin with financial support. We will instead have a letter-writing relationship. Pledges have determined what the income will be. Vision is pushed down to accommodate the money.

In churches where vision follows money there is no incentive to dream dreams. There is no expectation that we will ever need to reach out. Stagnation is quite acceptable. We will, of course, once again cut whatever we have to cut to make sure we stay solvent. It is a given that the fiscal health of the church will never be threatened. We know that. We know that we will take good care of ourselves. We just won't extend ourselves for others. The dollar amount of our pledges will be the fiscal police, keeping everything under control.

A church does not come alive until its leadership completely rethinks the vision/money relationship. The remainder of this chapter will define what this means. For now, imagine what is happening in a church with no stewardship campaign. The defining reality is what the ruling board leads the congregation to see as its vision for the coming year. There are no "pledge traps" to drag it down. The proposed budget is the set budget. Period. The congregation rallies together and gives generously to meet the vision. What these churches have discovered, and even we cowards can discover as well, is the liberating truth that money will indeed follow vision if we only give vision a chance.

2. An important step toward becoming a "money follows vision" church is to measure success in future terms. This is a reversal of common practice, where we evaluate ourselves solely in terms of the past. For example, last year's stewardship campaign produced pledges of $100,000, and then this year's campaign produced $105,000. We feel good. We had an increase of 5 percent. We define ourselves in glowing terms. The committee is thanked for raising more money than last year's campaign, and the 5-percent number is hailed as one of the largest increases in recent years. The stewardship chair saunters about during the coffee hour with an air of pride. Compared to the past, they did a fine job!

We certainly don't want to belittle the work done by the campaign committee, nor do we want to make light of how this church family has given its money in years past. Now let's be frank, at least with ourselves. In almost all churches we will find that $100,000 is a deplorable number, woefully below what the congregation should be doing given even a modicum of spiritual vitality. By evaluating from the past, we allow the church to use a deplorable number as their baseline. So the deplorable number is accepted as a given. To the congregation an increase in giving over that number feels like a healthy improvement. And so the family celebrates.

But with a future perspective we do not let $100,000 be the baseline. We know that 5 percent over deplorable is dreadful. We know that, rather than being a cause for us to jump up and down and clap our hands, it is reason to hang our heads in shame.

So as not to hurt feelings, we don't say these things just now about our immediately concluded campaign. We have the wisdom to wait until the planning stage of the next campaign. At that time our main objective will be to help the church think in terms of the future rather than the past. "What will happen when people really grow in their faith? What will our church be like when people begin to take giving seriously?" Suppose our members take seriously the notion of giving a percentage of their income to the local church, and suppose they only go to half a tithe—5 percent. Why, our giving would be $250,000! Let's start thinking about where we are going instead of where we have been. Let's unlock our thinking, so that $100,000 ceases to appear normal. In fact, it does not appear on our scene at all. Now $250,000 is normal for us. The future beckons us.

3. With one exception, which we will discuss shortly, churches with stewardship campaigns should not let the proposed budget be a part of their presentation. We often feel pressure to send out a detailed budget before expecting to receive pledges. "How will I know what to give if I don't know what I'm giving to?" Members demand to see numbers. They accuse us of having no business sense if we don't print up a budget prior to asking for pledges.

Our challenge is to resist yielding to the demand for a budget. Some vague pie charts to illustrate our overall priorities are acceptable. General comments building enthusiastic support for such specifics as the new youth worker or the relationship with that church in the third world can also be very helpful. Interpretive materials highlighting the positive work being done by and through the church is a very good tool for building family cohesion.

The real reason we do not use a detailed budget when asking for pledges is that doing so gives the false impression that we are running a fund-raising campaign and that people are giving to support the projected budget. That is just not what we are about. Our church is not about fund-raising. People do not "support the budget." Giving is to be about stewardship. It is our response to our Lord's gracious commitment to us. The great hymn "When I Survey the Wondrous Cross" ends with the line "love so amazing, so divine, demands my soul, my life, my all." The best argument for continuing stewardship campaigns is that they provide the church family an opportunity to act out their commitment to Jesus in a tangible way. In other words, the determinative question is not whether the proposed budget deserves my financial support. The question is whether Jesus has become Lord of my life in a way that elicits a significant response. Not presenting a detailed budget is a reminder to the whole church that stewardship is not fund-raising. In fact, one savvy observer of church life has said that the stewardship campaign is the way mainline congregations do revivals.

Another reason for not presenting a detailed budget is quite practical. People will see our budget projection and realize it calls for a 15 percent increase over last year. Fifteen percent immediately becomes the increase people are expected to give. It also becomes the ceiling defining how much people will increase. Since some givers cannot or will not increase by 15 percent, and others have died or left the church, and the perceived need to increase by 15 percent is met only by a few of the members, a 15 percent asked-for increase will usually result in about a 6 percent increase.

It is far better to convey the message that our vision is not a 15 percent increase—our vision is a spiritually renewed congregation. Our vision is some people increasing their giving by 1,000 percent, others tripling or doubling their giving. Never, never, never present a detailed budget in advance of the campaign.

4. We would do well to rethink the word "pledge." Colleagues have argued with me that "pledge" is the only word to use, because it connotes a commitment at the very time when churches make such low demands on anyone. They argue that forsaking the word "pledge" caters to the consumer mind-set that shops instead of committing. To these colleagues, questioning the word "pledge" is akin to selling out. My experience has been that pledges per se lead to unnecessary problems. I've known many persons who lower their pledge because a "pledge" sounds like a legal contract that must be met. Afraid that their household situation might not permit them to pay off their pledge, they enter only as high a number as they are sure to meet. "Pledges" tend to lower giving to a safe number.

I much prefer to use the term "Estimate of Giving." I like it for several reasons. It allows us to teach that the budgeting process is not an exact science. It is an art form. We estimate. We do not pin down. The word "estimate" means that no one is locked in. If someone's situation turns sour, he or she is not obligated to pay up. Nor should our members fail to realize that, if their situation improves, they are indeed allowed to give much more. All an "esti-mate" says is that this is the amount we anticipate giving. My experience is that giving goes up when churches shift their terminology from "pledge" to "estimate of giving."

In a church I served some years ago, a man had a very successful business. His stewardship card recorded annually a number in the $15,000 to $20,000 range. One fall he told me that his business was going through a tough time. He would not be able to pay his "pledge" and felt the responsible thing to do would be to cut his pledge dramatically for the next year. He hoped his busi-ness would turn around, but he wasn't sure when.

I told him we had no legally binding "pledges" in this church. We asked people to respond to Jesus with hope. He hoped his business would turn around. Why not anticipate that business would improve and "estimate" giv-ing on the basis of hope? Besides, church families have a way of rising to meet their collective anticipations for themselves. (A colleague told me the finan-cial administrator at his church had made a $30,000 miscalculation of pledges, allowing the budget to be set $30,000 higher than it should have been. Miraculously, over the year the church rose to the occasion, and with-out being aware of the mistake simply gave $30,000 more.) So I invited my friend whose business was struggling to "estimate" a hopeful number. He wrote his usual number on the card. His business did not make a comeback that year, but the congregation covered him and met its budget. So let's not get hung up about "pledges." Let's call them what they are: "estimates."

5. Another way to ease a congregation beyond the "pledge trip" is to remind people that we permit a changeable budget. Some churches fail to respond to great opportunity in September because they locked in their bud-get for the year the previous January. By this reasoning the church is allowed to have creative thoughts only once every year, at budget-setting time, and we all know that this is not a very openly creative time.

Speaking for my own denomination, our ruling board sets the budget, and they can change the budget any time they want. Building the level of trust and insight required to enable a ruling board to assume responsibility for such flexibility takes time. Perhaps it will help to spend some time reflecting with them on an aspect of last year's budget that exceeded that budget, and dis-cussing the good that was done by that overrun. Buying the new copier blew the administration budget to smithereens, but our ministry is greatly helped by having it. It was worth it. Fiscal flexibility happened, and, behold, it was good.

6. Earlier we mentioned that at stewardship time we are wise not to pub-lish a proposed budget, with one exception. That exception is mission. Here

a specific dollar amount or a specific percentage is helpful. As has been noted in another chapter, mission usually gets cut when the budgeting debates occur. It is treated like a fifth wheel. The mission line of a church budget is a bean counter's delight, because it can be reduced on a whim to make all the other numbers balance.

When we say that money follows vision, we are talking about a vision that is rooted in spiritual renewal and mission, which dares to take risks to see that mission is a serious player at the center of a church's life.

Spiritually alive people are generous people. Spiritually alive people expect to see a link between their response to Jesus Christ and the work of Jesus Christ in the world. When the ruling board of a church declares itself serious about mission, spiritually alive and generous people respond. The more specific the mission need, the more generous the response. I have not yet seen a legitimate need put before a church where the congregation did not rise up to meet that need.

What I am suggesting is that at the church we are serving we work to a point where we are ready to go for it. We are ready to act on the belief that in this congregation our vision of mission rules. Money follows.

Two episodes: Our church had been through the stewardship campaign. The heads of all committees and organizations with a line item in the budget had had their sit-down on a Saturday morning to gore one another's oxen. Budgets had been pruned. Even the mission committee had volunteered to postpone a project until the next year, dropping their budget slightly.

When the smoke cleared, we were still more than $110,000 in the hole. The mission committee still had a significant increase and continued to be a substantial part of the whole budget. For this reason, the following Tuesday evening when the mission committee was holding its monthly meeting in the church lounge they were fully prepared for "the visit" an hour or so into their meeting from the finance committee, which had its own meeting at the same time in the church library. It was the finance committee's task to draft a budget to be presented to the ruling board. The assumption was that again "business as usual" would prevail. The budget would be balanced by lopping more than $110,000 off the mission line.

It happened that I had been at that church long enough to shoot my mouth off. So I shared two of my philosophies of church finance with the stern saints poring over their budget sheets. First, even with the most thorough of stewardship campaigns, we have only the vaguest idea how much income the church will have in the coming year. The more dynamic the church, the greater the margin of error. Praise God! What this means is that balancing a budget to the penny is a waste of everyone's time and indicates a personality type that is no friend to venturing forth in trust. So I suggested we not worry about trying to have a budget that balanced.

Secondly, I told them I am a believer in the pastor's knowing what people give to the church. I also explained that after I had begun the practice of reviewing the estimate-of-giving cards, I figured out one of the reasons why I did it. Persons who were generous in their giving tended in disproportionate numbers to accept risk as a necessary component of faith. They also tended to be very supportive of mission. Givers are visionary people.

To the argument that people would withhold their money if we approved a deficit budget, I countered with an argument of my own. I told the committee that I knew where the money came from in that church. It came from people with a heart for mission. I advised them that generosity from our most mission-conscious parishioners supported not only mission but many non-mission areas of the budget as well. To cut mission so that our ledger statement looked neater would, in fact, be the bigger (and less responsible) risk, in that it would offend our biggest supporters. Since money comes from supporters, we would be taking a responsible and more than acceptable risk going for the whole enchilada on mission and asking the ruling board to pass a budget $110,000 in the red.

That's just what we did. To my surprise, the finance committee voted unanimously and then the ruling board voted overwhelmingly to approve the deficit budget. Sometimes these Smythes amaze me.

Immediately two things happened. Many of our members became apoplectic. Their rage at such fiscal irresponsibility was vented in letters, tirades, and long harangues, especially, I am told, at local dinner parties. At the same time, a second and more important phenomenon occurred. Our givers gave. Without our even asking for it, $70,000 in extra gifts came in the week after we announced the deficit, and we finished the year $45,000 in the black.

The Tuesday evening when the finance committee had met, it was a joy to walk down to the mission committee for "the visit" an hour into their meeting and tell them the news. I walked into a room filled with people braced for budgetary surgery. I walked out of a room filled with enthusiastic people still somewhat dazed by the news, thankful to be in the visionary church of Jesus Christ.

The second episode has happened often, and is, I hope, becoming routine in the church I now serve. Most of us in ministry soon learn that the budget has "fixed" items and it has "flexible" items. The electric bill is "fixed." The personnel budget is basically "fixed," with a small "flexible" amount for possible raises in salary. Supplies, insurance, and heat are "fixed." Mission is "flexible," depending on what we have left over after the "fixed" items are lined up against projected income.

At some point a still small voice within us begins to question the spiritual integrity of budgeting this way. The voice nags at us. "Who says the fixed work of Christ's church is cups for the coffee hour and electricity for all our computers?" "Who says feeding the hungry, housing the homeless, or teaching the illiterate to read are flexible items, only included if we have resources left over?" "Shouldn't all this be reversed?" "Shouldn't feeding the hungry be our fixed budget item and buying cups and brewing coffee for our coffee hour be flexible?" "In fact how could we have fallen so far from discipleship in our churches that the matter even needs to be raised?"

The still small voice is compelling.

A friend of mine once offered what I thought was a profound insight. He wondered aloud: "If we who set the budget for the church are not disciplined in our giving, setting our gifts to others first, how can we ask the families in the congregation to discipline themselves and set their gift to the church first?"

So, to return to what we were saying at the outset of this chapter, we do not hold up budget numbers at stewardship time except in one area—mission. The ruling board sets the mission budget ahead of the stewardship campaign and declares it "fixed." All else is "flexible," depending on how we decide to budget after estimates are in. This procedure has been followed in at least two churches, and the response has been remarkable. People warm to vision. Generous people become even more generous when that vision is mission. A church that risks its fiscal security to follow Jesus is a church we need and want to support.

Can you believe it? The Smythe family who were once total strangers to us are not only embracing us as family. They are mobilizing themselves for mission. It has taken a lot of time and prayerful encouragement, but their commitment to mission and vision for how mission can happen is really quite amazing.

Conclusion

*I*n 1993, I cochaired the ministers' committee for a Billy Graham Crusade at the late great Three Rivers Stadium in Pittsburgh. Our church got on board in a big way. We had a large steering committee. We were a host church for a series of training events. Our in-congregation advertising was extensive. We sent a large number of parishioners, including my wife, to sing in the choir. We signed up ushers and counselors; people became part of the prayer team. Persons promised to bring friends. I did pulpit announcements every Sunday for what seemed like a decade. We chartered buses and brought scores of people to the stadium for what I had promised would be one of the high points of people's lives: a chance to hear a man who is arguably the most significant preacher of the twentieth century.

Opening night we must have had twenty-five to thirty thousand people in the stands. The podium was on a platform out behind second base. The dais was filled with Christian dignitaries. Some were from the Graham organization, some were famous Americans who had given their lives to Jesus Christ. The choir numbered in the thousands. When they sang, it was powerful and moving. I eagerly awaited a chance to hear Dr. Graham deliver what I knew would be a stem-winder of a sermon.

When the time for the sermon came, I remembered that Dr. Graham had been ill. He was suffering from Parkinson's disease, and we knew that the very act of walking to the pulpit would be a labor of love on his part. We had worried that his failing health might even prevent him from being able to make it to Pittsburgh at all. The whole venture was an act of faith on the part of many people. Here he was, standing straight and tall in the pulpit, his image telecast on the giant screen atop the stands in what would be dead center field at a baseball game. His famous voice resonated through the loudspeaker system. All seemed well. Billy Graham was preaching.

As he moved into his remarks, I breathed a sigh of relief. Whatever ailments were tormenting his body, they all seemed to be controlled by the Spirit of the living God, as Dr. Graham had a full command of his faculties. His voice was strong, his thought process sharp, his material clear. I had heard most of his stabs at humor before, but I laughed politely and sensed others were doing the same. His statistics about the world situation showed a person who was pastor to the whole globe. Little of it was new, however, and none of it caused me to take out a pen and paper to record his gems for some future sermon of my own.

Then a terrible thought began to creep into my mind. I pushed it out of my consciousness the first several times I thought it. It kept coming back. Finally, I could not deny what I was thinking—I had to face my own insight: This really is not a very good sermon. Now I know that as a preacher I am a tough audience. I'll admit it. I really don't like to listen to sermons. They bore me; they bring out the worst of my critical nature. I'm convinced the Lord called me to be a preacher, realizing that making me a preacher would be about the only way to get me into a sanctuary at sermon time. I tried to deny my judgments about Dr. Graham's message by blaming my own hypercritical attitude, but even that didn't work. Clearly, I was listening to a "nice" but obvious message that was too much of a rehash of what I already knew, being delivered in an obvious way.

Then I began to be concerned about the many people I had convinced to be in the stands. They might never trust my invitation again. They might be so disappointed that they would not come the next night. They might hold it against me and our church. I felt embarrassed, disappointed, fearful of having the whole crusade collapse.

About seventeen minutes into the sermon I had pretty well decided I would have to do a lot of explaining to the people who had come to the crusade in our buses. Eighteen minutes into the sermon I hoped Dr. Graham would find some way to save the sermon. Nineteen minutes into it I realized he was not going to salvage this one. It was a lost cause. At about minute twenty I slumped back into my seat, resigned to the fact that Billy Graham was not the stem-winder of a preacher I had hoped he was. I am ashamed to admit it. As I crossed my arms over my chest in hopelessness, the actual thought whirling in my mind was, The old boy has lost his fastball. He doesn't have it anymore. I tuned out Billy Graham twenty minutes into his sermon.

Then an odd thing happened. The words blaring through the loudspeaker began to get to the core of my soul. In a very private way, behind all my professional concerns about the night being a fiasco, I found myself feeling as if I were the only person in Three Rivers Stadium. I was invited to look at my life from an eternal perspective. My sinfulness and my hopelessness again bubbled to the surface of my consciousness, as they had in the past at moments when I was ripe to hear the gospel. My Lord and Savior Jesus was being talked about in ways that awoke those corners of my faith that had dozed off to slumber in recent years. I found myself enthused, filled anew with God's grace. I was swept up in the life-giving thrill of having Jesus as my Savior.

I heard a voice inviting people to get up out of their seats and come forward. Somehow this invitation clicked my mind back to that early summer's night and the stadium full of people. I prayed for the people who were going forward. I prayed for their counselors. I offered my own prayer of gratitude for my faith, for my salvation, for my call to lead God's people. While I recalled that I wasn't so sure Billy Graham could still preach, I knew that I had been taken to the heavens that night and had had a personal meeting with the One before whom every knee shall bow and every tongue confess that this Jesus is Lord. I left Three Rivers Stadium, searched for and found the bus, and got on for the ride back home, not altogether sure what had just happened.

Being a moderately inquisitive chap and having enough attention deficit not to be able to sit all the way through crusade services two nights in a row, I decided the next night to stroll through the labyrinthine corridors of the stadium. I dropped in on various locations of backstage crusade action. Stopping by the prayer room, my eyes were opened. A sheet of paper explained it all. I took one from the pile of printed materials on a table by the door. There on a minute-by-minute schedule was the prayer list, explaining not only what was to be happening at that very instant out on the podium behind second base but also what we were to pray for the Lord to be doing in and through that part of the crusade.

The prayer sheet told us when Dr. Graham would be starting his sermon. Are you ready for this? They explicitly singled out the first twenty minutes of his message for only one purpose: to get Dr. Graham out of the way. Evidently, the Graham ministry had realized that while the crowd is focused on the ability and fame of Billy Graham they are not thinking about Jesus. So backstage at each crusade dozens of people are on their knees praying that by about twenty minutes into the sermon, the people will have stopped paying attention to the preacher so that they can give their attention to the preacher's Lord.

That was it. Billy Graham had no interest in wowing me with his preaching skills. He really did not care if I thought he was a good preacher or not. In fact, he probably prayed that I would give up on his oratorical skills. It was the goal of the Graham ministry to have me and thousands seated around me forget Billy Graham by about the twenty-minute mark and let Jesus come center stage from then on. You see the point. Billy Graham has become one of the most significant preachers of the twentieth century because he has had no interest in being one of the most significant preachers of the twentieth century. He has just wanted to be a faithful servant of his Lord.

What a lesson for us all!

John the Baptist was told by his followers that a preacher named Jesus had come to town and was attracting some of John's disciples. Institutional success seemed in jeopardy. John's reputation as the hottest game in town was slipping. Surely, John would employ some technique to win the crowd back to himself. He did not. Instead he said of Jesus, "He must increase, but I must decrease" (John 3:30).

I can think of no better way to send us forward than that. Ours is a profession where too often we are made the issue or we make ourselves the issue. We spend lots of useless energy trying to be "good," to be "well received," to "increase." We arrive at a Smythe family reunion of a church and tell them we are too important to help them set up the picnic tables. We are too smart and well educated to listen to their silly ideas about how baptism should be done. Then we wonder why our ministry is so frustrated. We fail to serve our Lord because we take ourselves too seriously. We forget that we have been called not to be the best and the brightest, but to be a fool for Christ.

Dr. Graham's prayers were answered. Twenty minutes into his sermon I had let myself believe that Billy Graham wasn't anything special, just as he planned. By the end of the evening I found myself in the presence of an awesome God, who is very special. "The Lord must increase, but I must decrease." It's not a bad way to do ministry.